Edexcel GCSE

English and English Language

Core

Student Book

Rachael Smith
Pat West
Danuta Reah
Consultant: **Geoff Barton**

A PEARSON COMPANY

Contents

Introduction

From Martin Phillips

Welcome to Edexcel English! We've worked hard to plan this course to make English engaging and exciting and to design assessments that really help you to show the skills you have developed.

Whether you're taking GCSE English or English Language you will have the opportunity to read and write texts about issues that are relevant to the world around you and to study both printed and on-screen texts, such as podcasts, trailers and websites. We expect you to have a personal opinion about all sorts of things you read and to be able to back up your opinion by giving good examples from the text. You have to write interestingly and engagingly in different genres and we also expect you to be able to both speak and listen in a variety of contexts.

This book has been designed to help you to get the best possible grade in GCSE English or English Language. It's tailored to helping students achieve grades D to B and is full of tasks that will help you to get better at doing these various parts of English. We have tried to make these activities enjoyable and interesting and we hope they will encourage you to carry on reading, writing and communicating long after your GCSE English is done and dusted, as well as helping you to get a good grade in your GCSE.

Good luck with your studies and I hope you get the best possible results!

Martin Phillips

Martin Phillips, Senior Examiner for GCSE English

The Edexcel GCSE English and English Language specifications

Although GCSE English and GCSE English Language are separate qualifications, the Unit 1 controlled assessment task is common to both, and there are other common elements, including Speaking and Listening, and both have a practical writing task in the Unit 2 examination. Here is an overview of the specifications for both GCSE English and GCSE English Language:

Unit 1 English Today (English and English Language)	
Controlled Assessment **What is this unit worth?** 20% of the total marks **How long do students have?** 4 hours (2 hours for each task) **What is the first task?** Reading response to two on-screen or printed non-fiction texts on the same theme	**What is the Reading task worth?** 10% of the total marks **What is the second task?** One non-fiction writing task on the same theme as the reading texts **What is the Writing task worth?** 10% of the total marks
Unit 2 The Writer's Craft (English)	**Unit 2 The Writer's Voice (English Language)**
Exam **What is this unit worth?** 40% of the total marks **How long is the exam?** 2 hours **What is Section A?** One three-part question based on an extract from a Shakespeare play you have studied **What is Section A worth?** 10% of the total marks **What is Section B?** One three-part question based on an extract from a Different Cultures novel you have studied **What is Section B worth?** 10% of the total marks **What is Section C?** One practical writing task **What is Section C worth?** 20% of the total marks	Exam **What is this unit worth?** 40% of the total marks **How long is the exam?** 1 hour 45 minutes **What is Section A?** One question on the language features of a non-fiction text or Different Cultures novel you have studied **What is Section A worth?** 25% of the total marks **What is Section B?** One practical writing task **What is Section B worth?** 15% of the total marks
Unit 3 Creative English (English)	**Unit 3 Spoken Language (English Language)**
Controlled Assessment **What is this unit worth?** 40% of the total marks **How long do students have?** Up to 4 hours for the poetry reading task and the creative writing task (2 hours for each task) **What is the first task?** Speaking and listening tasks: communicating and adapting language, interacting and responding, and creating and sustaining roles **What are the Speaking and Listening tasks worth?** 20% of the total marks **What is the second task?** A poetry reading task drawing on one literary heritage poem and at least two poems from the Anthology **What is the Poetry Reading task worth?** 10% of the total marks **What is the third task?** A creative writing task in response to a stimulus (e.g. an image, video clip or podcast) **What is the Creative Writing task worth?** 10% of the total marks	Controlled Assessment **What is this unit worth?** 40% of the total marks **How long do students have?** Up to 4 hours for the spoken language study task and the writing for the spoken voice task (2 hours for each task) **What is the first task?** Speaking and listening tasks: communicating and adapting language, interacting and responding, and creating and sustaining roles **What are the Speaking and Listening tasks worth?** 20% of the total marks **What is the second task?** A spoken language study based on two examples of spoken language **What is the Spoken Language Study worth?** 10% of the total marks **What is the third task?** One writing for the spoken voice task **What is the Writing for the Spoken Voice task worth?** 10% of the total marks

Introduction

How is the book structured?

This book is divided into five units, each of which corresponds to one of the units in the English or English Language specification. Units 1 and 2 of this book are common to both GCSE English and GCSE English Language.

Specification	Unit	This book covers ...
English and English Language	Unit 1 English Today: Reading	the non-fiction Reading controlled assessment task.
	Unit 1 English Today: Writing	the non-fiction Writing controlled assessment task.
	Unit 2 The Writer's Craft / The Writer's Voice	the writing task in the exam (Section C of English and Section B of English Language).
English only	Unit 3 Creative English	the creative writing controlled assessment task.
English Language only	Unit 3 Spoken Language	the Spoken Language Study and the Writing for the Spoken Voice controlled assessment tasks.

Each unit is broken down into lessons, each of which opens with its own learning objectives. These introduce the skills, and are followed by teaching and stepped activities that help you develop the skills you need to achieve grades D to B.

There are some activities that refer to additional digital resources, such as videos and podcasts, which are available on the ActiveTeach CD-ROM that accompanies this student book. These are to help you prepare for the options in the specifications for Unit 1 English Today and Unit 3 Creative English that require you to respond to or produce digital texts.

Assessment Practice

At intervals throughout each unit there are Assessment Practice activities that allow you to tackle an exam-style question or part of a controlled assessment task. These are followed by ResultsPlus Maximise your marks pages which provide sample student answers to the question you have attempted with examiner comments. You can read these before or after you grade your own response to the assessment practice in the ResultsPlus: Self-assessment activity.

Regular ResultsPlus activities help students understand what they need to do to improve their grades.

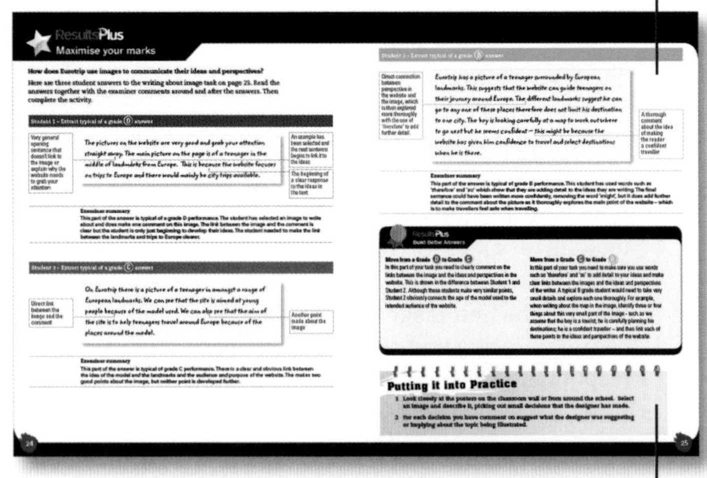

Putting it into Practice activities suggest tasks you could complete to reinforce the skills you have learned.

At the end of each unit is a sample controlled assessment task or exam paper, so that you can see how you will be assessed. Mark schemes for these are available in the corresponding Teacher Guide. On the ActiveTeach CD-ROM there are interactive ResultsPlus grade improvement activities that include extracts from student responses at each band, with activities that help you to understand the differences between the bands and what you need to do to achieve better results.

ResultsPlus

These features combine expert advice and guidance from examiners to show you **how to achieve better results.** Many are based on insight gained from how students have performed in past assessments.

Build better answers – These give you an exam-style question or part of a controlled assessment task and help you to understand the mark scheme against which you will be assessed. They explain what you need to do in your response to the task to achieve the marks in each band. This book will show you what you need to do to achieve a mark in Band 2, 3 or 4 in your controlled assessment tasks and a mark in Band 1, 2 or 3 in the Higher Tier exam.

Look at this part of a controlled assessment task: **Explore how the writers communicate their ideas and perspectives.**

■ A Band 2 answer will have **some exploration** of the ideas in the text but may not comment on these in a lot of detail. The answer will give very general points.

● A Band 3 answer will **clearly explore** the ideas and perspectives of the writer and will develop these to include **some specific** points with **appropriate examples**.

▲ A Band 4 answer will include a **thorough exploration** of the ideas and perspectives of the writers. It is likely to give a selection of **detailed and appropriate examples** to support the points being made.

Self assessment – These help you to check your answers to activities to make sure that you have demonstrated the skills you will need to show in your assessment. The self assessment features that follow Assessment Practice activities give you the opportunity to grade your answer using the mark scheme.

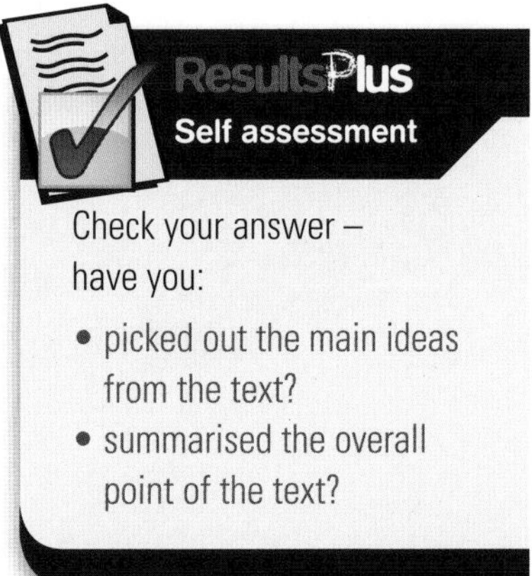

Check your answer – have you:

- picked out the main ideas from the text?
- summarised the overall point of the text?

Maximise your marks – These pages show examples of student work that is typical of what might be produced by students whose overall performance was at a grade D, C or B. Some of these examples are taken from real student work from the Edexcel GCSE English pilot. These examples should help you to understand what you need to do to achieve your target grade.

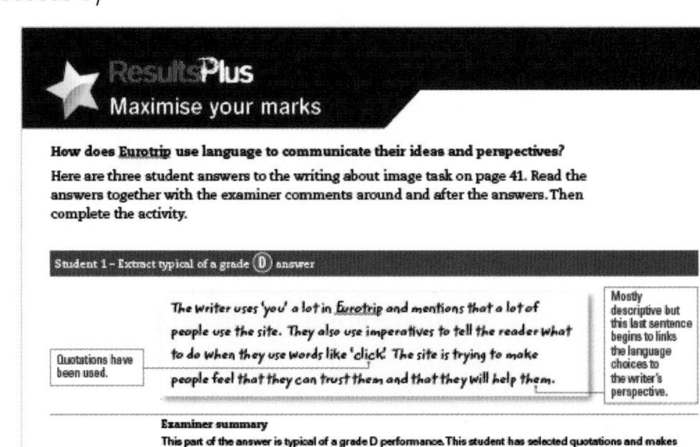

How does Eurotrip use language to communicate their ideas and perspectives?

Here are three student answers to the writing about image task on page 41. Read the answers together with the examiner comments around and after the answers. Then complete the activity.

Student 1 – Extract typical of a grade (D) answer

The writer uses 'you' a lot in Eurotrip and mentions that a lot of people use the site. They also use imperatives to tell the reader what to do when they use words like 'click'. The site is trying to make people feel that they can trust them and that they will help them.

Quotations have been used.

Mostly descriptive but this last sentence begins to links the language choices to the writer's perspective.

Examiner summary

This part of the answer is typical of a grade D performance. This student has selected quotations and makes a good attempt at identifying the language chosen. There is a suggested link between the comment about wanting to trust the site and the use of imperatives and 'you', but it is not clearly made. The student could have used the word 'because' to show the connection between the language and the comment.

Exam tip and Controlled assessment tip – These provide examiner advice and guidance to help improve your results.

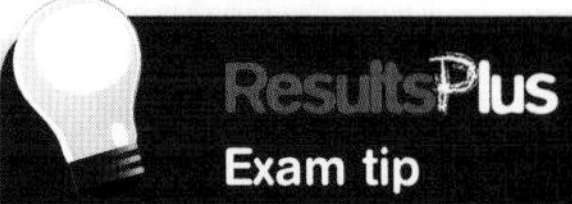

▲ In your examination, use between 10% and 20% of the time available thinking, planning and checking. Use the remaining 80%-90% writing your answer.

Watch out! – These warn you about common mistakes and misconceptions that examiners frequently see students make. Make sure that you don't repeat them!

■ Be careful not to merely state what the writers have said in their texts. Remember to focus on the *use* of image, presentation and language and *how* this reveals the writer's perspective.

Unit 1 English Today: Reading

Welcome to English Today, which is all about English in the world around you – the English you see and use every day of your life. In this student book, you will develop your skills in reading a range of non-fiction texts, some of them printed (such as posters, articles and reviews) and some of them on-screen (such as podcasts, trailers and websites).

This section of the book will help you to develop your reading skills, exploring how writers use presentation and language to communicate their ideas and perspectives to their readers. The texts and activities you will encounter in this book as you develop these skills are all focused on helping you to achieve your target grade in the reading part of your Unit 1 controlled assessment task.

Your assessment

Unit 1 is a controlled assessment unit. You will have two hours to complete one reading task. You can write up to 1000 words in your response to the task. The task will ask you to write about two different texts, on the same theme, from a choice of six. In order to prepare for your written response, you will have had the opportunity to study these texts in advance.

Your response to the task must show that you can:

- ✔ **make comparisons between two texts**
- ✔ **select appropriate details from the texts to support your ideas**
- ✔ **explore how writers use presentation and language to communicate their ideas and perspectives.**

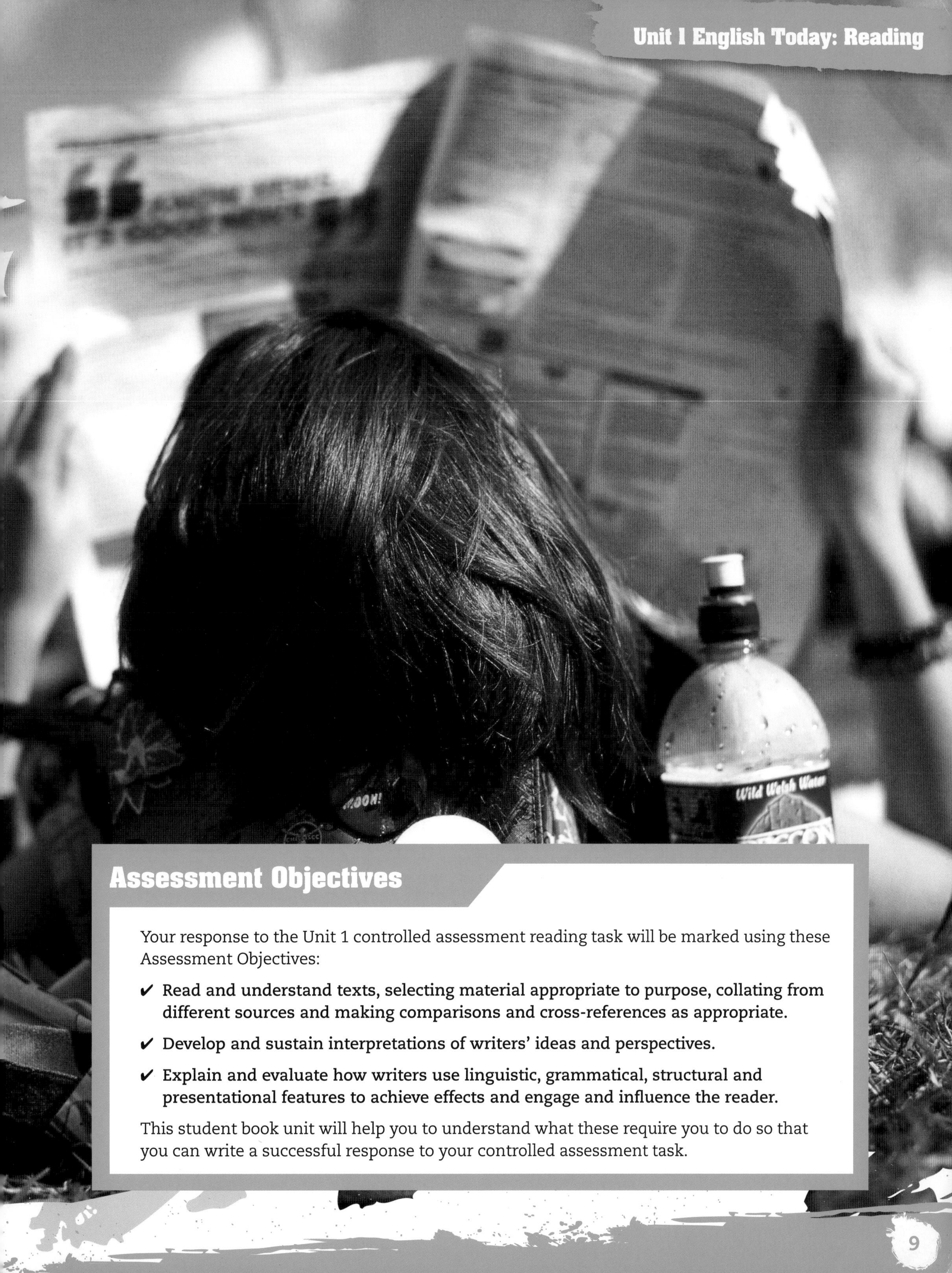

Assessment Objectives

Your response to the Unit 1 controlled assessment reading task will be marked using these Assessment Objectives:

- ✔ **Read and understand texts, selecting material appropriate to purpose, collating from different sources and making comparisons and cross-references as appropriate.**
- ✔ **Develop and sustain interpretations of writers' ideas and perspectives.**
- ✔ **Explain and evaluate how writers use linguistic, grammatical, structural and presentational features to achieve effects and engage and influence the reader.**

This student book unit will help you to understand what these require you to do so that you can write a successful response to your controlled assessment task.

1 Understanding main ideas

This lesson will help you to...

- → understand the main ideas a writer is communicating
- → summarise the key points of a text

Before you can tackle your controlled assessment task, you need to be confident that you understand the main ideas the writer is communicating in the texts you are writing about.

Texts can appear to be complicated when you first read them. Here are some strategies you can use to help you to work out the writer's main ideas:

- Work out the meaning of any word you don't understand by using **context** (looking at the other words in the sentence) or by using a dictionary.
- **Summarise** each paragraph or part of the text by writing a sentence summing it up in your own words.
- Highlight **key points** – these are the points the writer repeats or emphasises.

Activity 1

Read this text from the Bully Online website.

http://www.bullyonline.org

School Bully Online | Media Centre | Bully News | Resources

BULLYING AT WORK

Bullying is the common denominator of harassment, discrimination, prejudice, abuse, persecution, conflict and violence. When the bullying has a focus (eg race or gender) it is expressed as racial prejudice or harassment, or sexual discrimination and harassment, and so on. Although bullying often lacks a focus, bullies are deeply prejudiced but at the same time sufficiently devious to not reveal their prejudices to the extent that they contravene laws on harassment and discrimination.

I believe bullying is the single most important social issue of today, for the study of bullying provides an opportunity to understand the behaviours which underlie almost all conflict and violence.

Most of the information on this site is derived from experience of dealing with bullying in the workplace, however, much applies to bullying in schools, in relationships (eg domestic violence and family bullying), in uniform (armed services, police, prisons etc), in crime, with neighbours, and in abuse of the elderly.

1. **Try to use context clues to work out the meanings of any words you don't understand. For example:**

   'Persecution' might mean to pick on someone or treat them badly, as this is similar to abuse, conflict and violence.

2. **Write a one-sentence summary of each paragraph in your own words. For example:**

   Paragraph 1: Bullying causes lots of different types of bad behaviour...

3. **Pick out the key points from the website text.**

Once you have understood a text you need to be able to **summarise** clearly the ideas that the writer is communicating.

Look at this summary of the extract from the Bully Online website, which contains the main ideas from the text but expresses them in a shorter and more precise way.

Bullying is the cause of many different types of violent or harmful behaviour and it is an important issue because it affects lots of people in different situations.

Activity 2

Read this extract from a *Guardian* newspaper article about the social networking site Facebook.

1 **Use the strategies you have practised to help you to understand the text.**

2 **Write a sentence summarising the ideas that the writer is communicating.**

With friends like these...

Tom Hodgkinson

I despise Facebook. This enormously successful American business describes itself as "a social utility that connects you with the people around you". But hang on. Why on God's earth would I need a computer to connect with the people around me? Why should my relationships be mediated through the imagination of a bunch of supergeeks in California?

And does Facebook really connect people? Doesn't it rather disconnect us, since instead of doing something enjoyable such as talking and eating and dancing and drinking with my friends, I am merely sending them little ungrammatical notes and amusing photos in cyberspace, while chained to my desk? A friend of mine recently told me that he had spent a Saturday night at home alone on Facebook, drinking at his desk. What a gloomy image. Far from connecting us, Facebook actually isolates us at our workstations.

It also encourages a disturbing competitiveness around friendship: it seems that with friends today, quality counts for nothing and quantity is king. The more friends you have, the better you are. You are "popular", in the sense much loved in American high schools.

You may be asked to write about on-screen texts, such as videos and podcasts, in your controlled assessment task. To understand the main ideas in these types of text you will need to look at the images and listen carefully to the soundtrack chosen as well as the words.

Activity 3

Watch the video about teenage violence, from an episode of *Newsnight* on the ActiveTeach.

1 **List the key points the writer is making. Look at the visual images used and listen carefully to the narrator.**

2 **Look at your list of key points. What is the main idea the writer of this text wants the reader to understand? Try to summarise this in 15 words or fewer.**

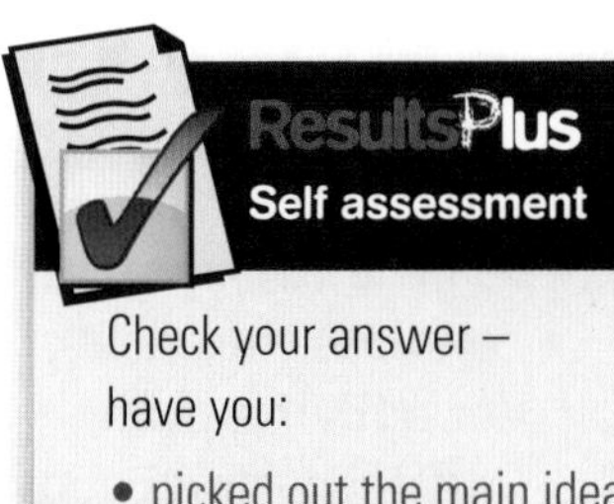

Check your answer – have you:

- picked out the main ideas from the text?
- summarised the overall point of the text?

2 Understanding the writer's perspective

This lesson will help you to...

- → identify the writer's perspective
- → understand how a writer communicates their perspective to a reader

You need to be able to work out the writer's **perspective** in the texts you are studying for your controlled asessment. The writer's perspective is their point of view on what they are writing about. The writer's perspective might be different from your own or other people's perspectives.

Activity 1

Read Greg's account and Darren's account of the same incident. Neither account is false, but the writer of each one has a different perspective.

Greg's account

It was awful. He hit me hard in the face and all his friends laughed at me when I started to cry. I was just walking past and was trying to be helpful by pointing out that the bell had gone. They always laugh at me in the corridor and I thought if I tried to help they would like me more. I don't understand what is going on.

Darren's account

This has nothing to do with my friends. They didn't even realise what had happened until after I hit him. I think they were laughing at a joke Jack had made. I did punch him but he told me I was going to be late with this smirk on his face like he was going to tell the teacher. I have never really seen him before and I thought he was trying to show me up in front of my friends. People seem to do that with me.

1. **Describe what happened in the corridor.**
2. **What might have influenced the two boys to view the events in such different ways? Write down your ideas.**
3. **Greg's perspective is that he has been bullied by this group for a long time. Write a sentence explaining what Darren's perspective is on Greg. Why is it important to have heard Darren's perspective?**

Writers can use more than words to suggest their perspective on an event. The way a writer uses presentation (such as font size or style) or still or moving images can also help you to work out their perspective.

Activity 2

These two posters explore the issue of bullying from different perspectives. For each poster:

1. **Write a sentence summarising the idea it communicates.**
2. **Describe from what perspective it explores the issue of bullying.**
3. **How does the writer show this perspective to the reader?**

Poster 1

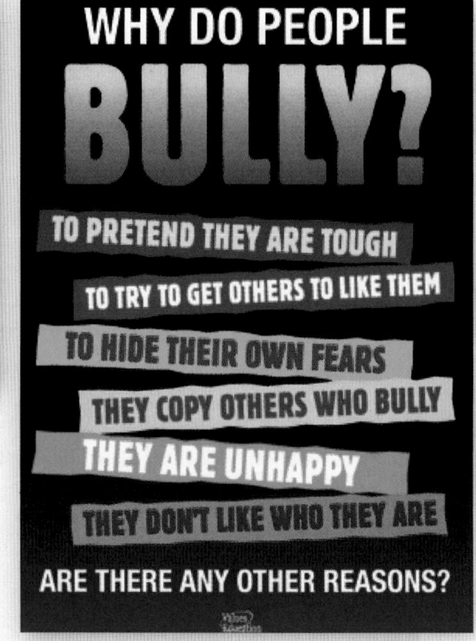

Poster 2

You can identify a writer's perspective by looking at the language the writer uses to present ideas. If a writer writes about a topic such as video games using negative words such as 'awful' or 'terrible' you know that their perspective is that they don't like them.

Activity 3

Read the newspaper article from the *Daily Mail* below about a computer game that deals with the subject of bullying.

OUTRAGE OVER 'SCHOOL BULLY' COMPUTER GAME

Campaigners are calling for a violent new computer game, in which gamers play a school bully, to be banned.

The aim of the PlayStation2 game is to terrorise the other pupils at a school. Players dish out beatings, throw stink bombs and give 'wedgies' by yanking at their underwear.

Game developer Rockstar Vancouver has already had to change the name following complaints about the original title – *Bully*. The game is now called *Canis Canem Edit*, which is Latin for Dog Eat Dog.

The game has already caused a major outcry in the US, with a protest in New York and condemnation from anti-bullying charities.

In the UK, campaigners including Labour MP Keith Vaz are now calling for it be to banned.

An insider at Rockstar Vancouver said: "The game gives kids the chance to misbehave at school and get away with it. "It might only be a computer game but there are lots of realistic elements."

Released at the end of this month, the sick game is expected to be another massive hit for the company which also created the lawless Grand Theft Auto series.

1 What does the headline make you think the writer's perspective will be?
2 Pick out the words from the article that help you to understand the writer's perspective.
3 Write a sentence summarising what the writer's perspective is on the computer game.

ResultsPlus
Watch out!

■ Be careful not to merely state what the writers have said in their texts. Remember to focus on the *use* of image, presentation and language and comment on *how* this reveals the writer's perspective.

ResultsPlus
Build better answers

Look at this part of a controlled assessment task: **Explore how the writers communicate their ideas and perspectives.**

■ A Band 2 answer will have **some exploration** of the writers' ideas but may not comment on these in a lot of detail. The answer will give very **general points**.

● A Band 3 answer will **clearly explore** the ideas and perspectives of the writer and will develop these to include some **specific points with appropriate examples**.

▲ A Band 4 answer will include a **thorough exploration** of the ideas and perspectives of the writers. It is likely to give a selection of **detailed and appropriate examples to support the points being made**.

3 Identifying audience and purpose 1

This lesson will help you to...

- → identify the audience of a text
- → identify the purpose of a text

In your controlled assessment task you will need to show how the writer has made the text appropriate for its audience and purpose. Identifying the audience of a text means working out who it is aimed at – who the reader, listener or viewer is likely to be. The audience can be described in many ways: whether they are male or female, young or old, an expert or a novice, and so on.

Activity 1

Look at the three magazine covers below.

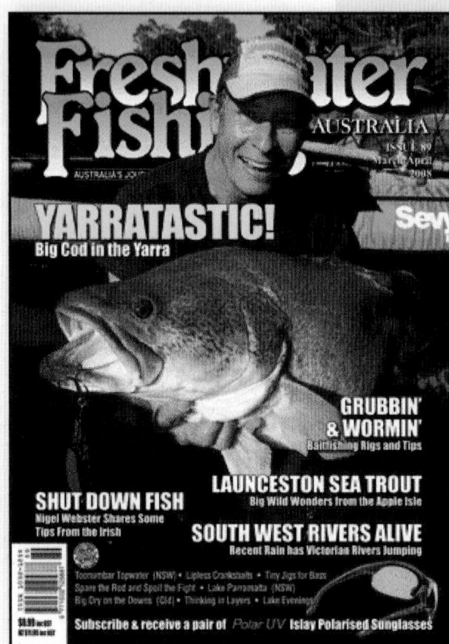

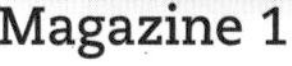

Magazine 1

Magazine 2

Magazine 3

1 **List the words you would use to describe the audience of each magazine. Think about whether each magazine is aimed at:**
   - men or women or both
   - a particular age group
   - people with particular interests or hobbies.

2 **For each of the magazines, write two or three sentences explaining what made you choose the words you did to describe its audience.**

Identifying the purpose of a text means working out why it has been written. There are many words you can use to describe a text's purpose, some of which are listed below. Remember that a text can have more than one purpose.

PURPOSE					
persuade	explain	imagine	argue	describe	advise
review	comment	inform	analyse	recount	entertain

Activity 2

1 Copy and complete the following table by placing the different purposes from the list on page 14 under one of the headings. An example has been done for you.

Keeping people up to date	Having an opinion	Helping people to see
inform		

2 Explain the choices you made. Did you place any of the purposes under more than one heading? Why?

Activity 3

Read these two texts, one is from a health website and the other is from a newspaper column in the *Guardian*.

No need to be a fitness fanatic

View all 200 topics

Featured topics

Alcohol
Cancer
Fitness
Good food
Lose weight
Mental health
Stop smoking

Shedding a few pounds, and looking and feeling better as a result, isn't rocket science. In fact, it's pretty simple: cut out fatty foods and fizzy drinks, and start exercising. If the thought of jogging round the block brings you out in a cold sweat, don't worry. There are plenty of other things you can do to lose weight and feel a whole lot healthier.

If you walk 10,000 steps a day you'll burn 500 calories. And as you need to burn 3,500 calories to lose 500g (1lb) of body fat, walking 10,000 steps each day will burn 500g of body fat a week.

Dancing is rubbish.

Overrated, sweaty, rubbish, rubbish, it's for people who feel attractive and people whose arms and legs don't jerk away from their bodies like mine do, like teenagers ashamed to be seen with their mums. It's not right and it's not OK, especially in public, a place where some of us eat. If one must dance, I'd hope one'd have the decency to do it alone in one's bedroom, where only the dolls and JLS posters are there to see. How dare Arlene attempt to inflict dance on us, we who are clumsy and shame-filled and heavy on our feet. Imagine the humiliation of a village forced to polka. Imagine the smell.

1 Draw two spider diagrams, one for each text. Write the purpose of each text in the centre of the spider diagram. Around the outside, write the clues that helped you to decide what the purpose of each text was.

4 Identifying audience and purpose 2

This lesson will help you to...

→ **comment on how writers make texts appropriate for an audience and purpose**

Writers make lots of choices to make their text appropriate for its audience and purpose. These include:

- selecting **images** (still and/or moving images)
- choosing forms of **presentation** (font size and style, colour, borders and other presentational devices)
- making **language choices**.

Activity 1

Look at the book cover below. Think carefully about the purpose and audience and make sure you explain your answers to the following questions fully.

1 Why do you think the writer chose to use cartoon images?

2 Why do you think the writer showed most of the children smiling?

3 Why has the writer selected mostly primary colours such as red, blue, and yellow?

4 Why has the writer chosen to use big, simple shapes containing a small amount of text?

5 Why has the writer chosen to use the words 'COOL' and 'amaze' in the text?

6 Why do you think the writer has used so many exclamation marks?

In some texts, the audience and purpose may not be easy to identify, but you can use the same approach to work them out.

Activity 2

Read the article below from an online news website.

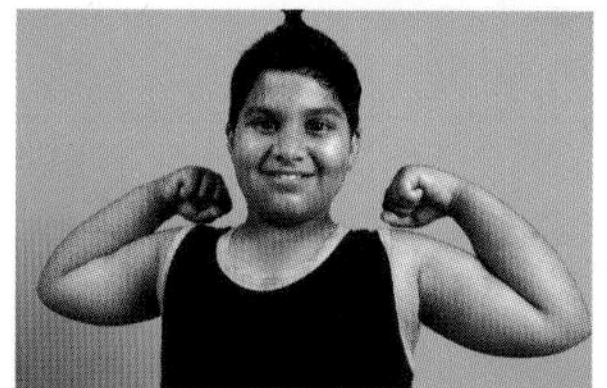

Fitness levels of school children

We asked the Carnegie research team to compare school children's fitness levels today with those of pupils 50 years ago. They measured the pupils' agility, endurance, power, speed and strength.

Activity	St Pauls School	1959	% Difference
Shuttle runs (in secs)	19	17	11.8
Sit ups (in 1 min)	24	25	4
Shoot the Cannon (in 1 min)	23	26	11.5
Skipping (in 1 min)	61	96	36.4
Press Ups	7	8	12.5
Run and Walk (in secs)	120	63	47.5
Standing Long Jump (in cm)	132	150	12
Target Throwing (out of 6)	3	6	50
Pull Ups	1	3	66.6

Title: Average Fitness Scores for school children in 2007 and 50 years ago
Source: Leeds Metropolitan University

1 Copy and complete the table to pick out the features that give you clues about the audience and purpose of this website.

	Images	Presentation	Language
Audience			
Purpose			

2 Using the information from your table, write a short paragraph explaining the audience and purpose of this website.

Check your answer – have you:

- clearly identified audience and purpose?
- identified features from the text to support your decision on the audience and purpose of the text?
- commented on how the writer has matched the text to the appropriate audience and purpose?

5 Understanding presentation

This lesson will help you to...

- → understand what presentational features and devices a writer can use
- → understand the impact of presentation on the reader

Your controlled assessment task will ask you to comment on how presentation is used to communicate ideas and perspectives. When a writer produces a text they think very carefully about the way that it is presented. They can use **presentational devices** to change the way the text looks, such as:

headings	text boxes	font size	font colour	bullet points	borders
images	numbering	font	shapes	background	captions

The first step when writing about presentation is to be able to identify the choices the writer has made.

Activity 1

Look carefully at the home page of the *Hollyoaks* website.

1 Find five examples of presentational devices used in the *Hollyoaks* website. Describe and comment on each of the presentational devices. For example:

The website has used purple boxes with white writing as headings on the website.

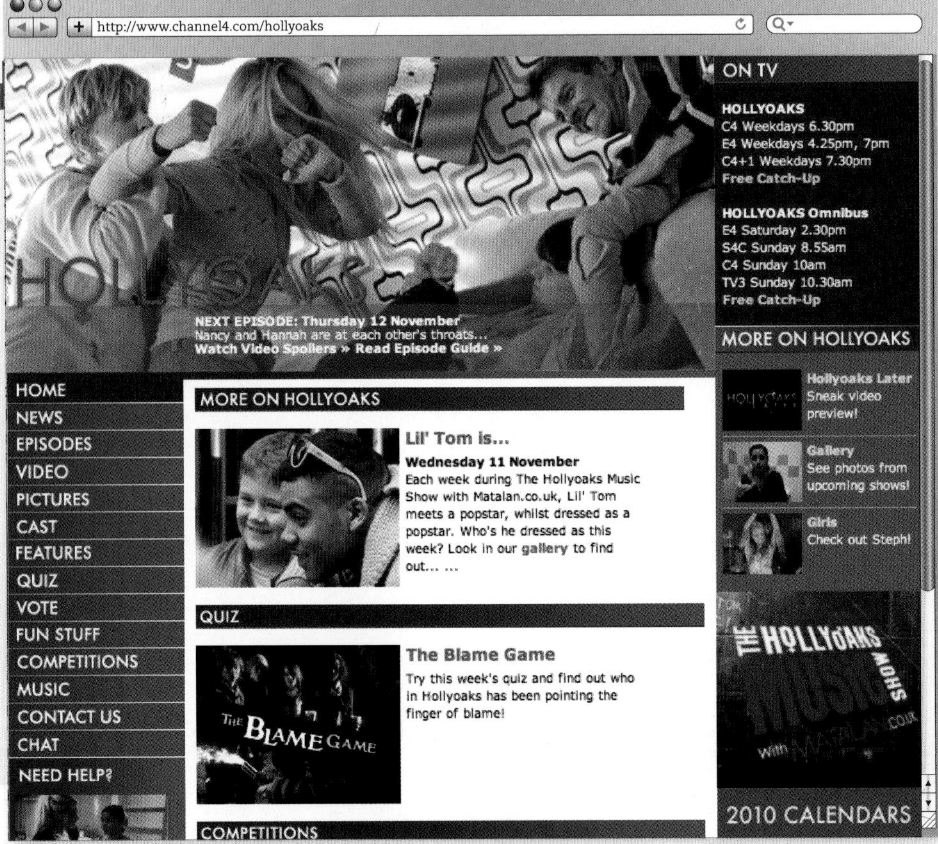

Presentational devices are used to have an impact on the audience. They also help to achieve the purpose of the text.

Activity 2

1 Who is the audience of the *Hollyoaks* website?

2 What is the purpose of the *Hollyoaks* website?

3 Look at the presentational devices you identified in Activity 1. How has the writer used these presentational devices to attract the audience and serve the purpose of the website?

You also need to be able to comment on the effect that presentational devices in the texts you are writing about have on a reader.

Activity 3

Look at the three different ways the word 'bang' is presented below:

BANG! **bang!** **BANG!**

1 **Describe the technique used to present the word each time and the effect this might have on the reader. For example:**

The use of capital letters for the word on the left makes it seem loud. Capital letters are often used for shouting in presentation, so this raises the volume.

2 **Identify a possible use of these texts from the presentational devices used. For example:**

The use of the graffiti style font makes the word on the right seem like the tag for a gang or a phrase that teenagers might use.

Activity 4

1 **Change how one of the following words or phrases is presented by using presentational devices such as font size, font style, bold text, underlining, colour and borders. Draw your design for your chosen word and explain the impact your presentational choices would have on a reader.**

Be quiet	Do it now	I love you
See you tomorrow	Come here	I want to go home

2 a) **Using a range of presentational devices, design the word 'Help' to show how it could be presented in:**

- **a charity leaflet appealing for money**
- **the home page of a magazine website.**

b) **Explain the different presentational choices you made for 'Help'. Explain how they help achieve the purpose and appeal to the two different audiences.**

ResultsPlus
Self assessment

Check your answer – have you:

- selected appropriate examples of presentation to comment on?
- commented on the impact of the presentation on the reader?
- explained how the presentation is appropriate to the audience and purpose of the text?

6 Exploring the effects of presentation

This lesson will help you to...

- → comment on the way presentational devices are used
- → explore the effects presentational devices create

When you are writing about the way a text is presented, you need to comment on how the presentation helps to achieve the text's purpose and appeal to its audience. You need to write about each presentational device used in your controlled assessment texts in turn and comment on how and why they have been used.

Look at the comments that have been made about one of the presentational devices used on the cover of the *Beano Max*.

identified one of the presentational devices used

At the bottom of the cover, the font looks like handwritten capitals to look as though the character from the Beano has written it. This reinforces the idea of the fast paced and mischievous antics suggested by the images.

commented on why this has been used

commented on how it has been used

Activity 1

Look again at the cover of the *Beano Max* above.

1 What is the purpose of this text and who is the audience? Explain your ideas.

2 Copy and complete the following table by commenting on how and why the presentational devices listed have been used.

Presentational device	How it has been used	Why it has been used
Logo		
Shapes		
Font colour		
Background		

3 Add to the table any other presentational devices you can find.

4 Using information from your table, write a paragraph explaining what ideas the presentation helps to communicate.

Activity 2

Now look at the science textbook below. The audience for this text is school children and its purpose is to inform and educate them about the environment and home energy resources.

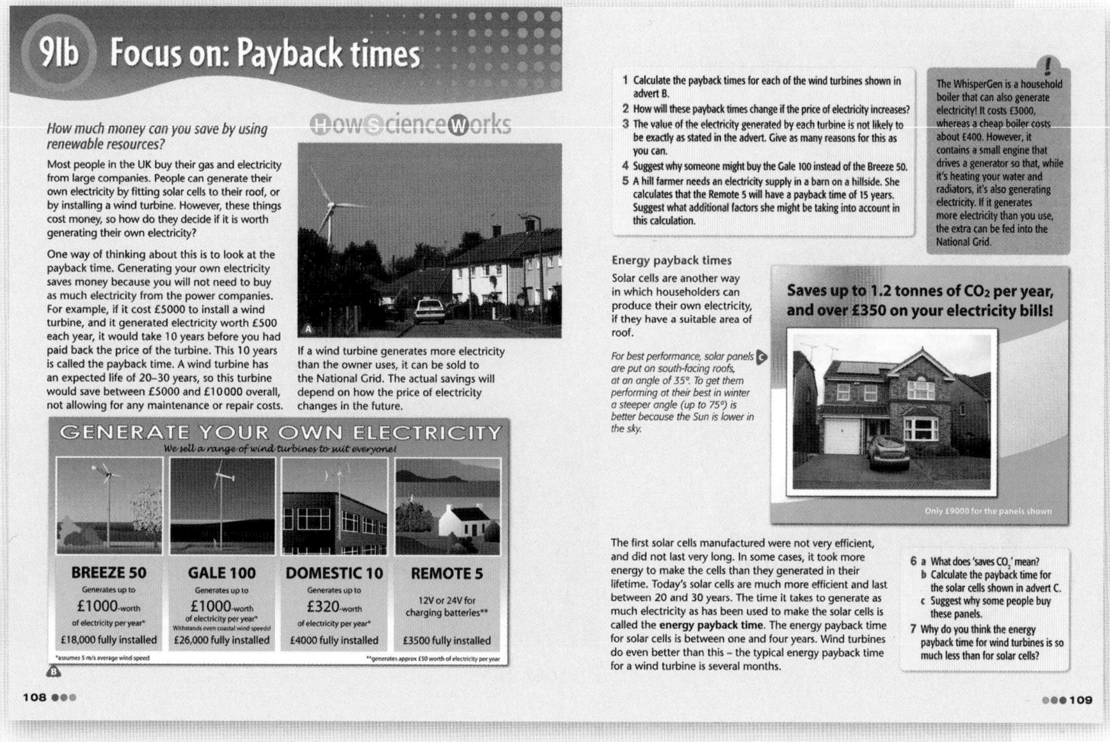

9Ib Focus on: Payback times

How Science Works

How much money can you save by using renewable resources?

Most people in the UK buy their gas and electricity from large companies. People can generate their own electricity by fitting solar cells to their roof, or by installing a wind turbine. However, these things cost money, so how do they decide if it is worth generating their own electricity?

One way of thinking about this is to look at the payback time. Generating your own electricity saves money because you will not need to buy as much electricity from the power companies. For example, if it cost £5000 to install a wind turbine, and it generated electricity worth £500 each year, it would take 10 years before you had paid back the price of the turbine. This 10 years is called the payback time. A wind turbine has an expected life of 20–30 years, so this turbine would save between £5000 and £10 000 overall, not allowing for any maintenance or repair costs.

A

If a wind turbine generates more electricity than the owner uses, it can be sold to the National Grid. The actual savings will depend on how the price of electricity changes in the future.

GENERATE YOUR OWN ELECTRICITY

We sell a range of wind turbines to suit everyone!

BREEZE 50	GALE 100	DOMESTIC 10	REMOTE 5
Generates up to £1000-worth of electricity per year*	Generates up to £1000-worth of electricity per year* Withstands even coastal wind speeds!	Generates up to £320-worth of electricity per year*	12V or 24V for charging batteries**
£18,000 fully installed	£26,000 fully installed	£4000 fully installed	£3500 fully installed

*assumes 5 m/s average wind speed

**generates approx £50 worth of electricity per year

B

108

1 Calculate the payback times for each of the wind turbines shown in advert B.
2 How will these payback times change if the price of electricity increases?
3 The value of the electricity generated by each turbine is not likely to be exactly as stated in the advert. Give as many reasons for this as you can.
4 Suggest why someone might buy the Gale 100 instead of the Breeze 50.
5 A hill farmer needs an electricity supply in a barn on a hillside. She calculates that the Remote 5 will have a payback time of 15 years. Suggest what additional factors she might be taking into account in this calculation.

!

The WhisperGen is a household boiler that can also generate electricity! It costs £3000, whereas a cheap boiler costs about £400. However, it contains a small engine that drives a generator so that, while it's heating your water and radiators, it's also generating electricity. If it generates more electricity than you use, the extra can be fed into the National Grid.

Energy payback times

Solar cells are another way in which householders can produce their own electricity, if they have a suitable area of roof.

For best performance, solar panels are put on south-facing roofs, at an angle of 35°. To get them performing at their best in winter a steeper angle (up to 75°) is better because the Sun is lower in the sky.

C

Saves up to 1.2 tonnes of CO_2 per year, and over £350 on your electricity bills!

Only £9000 for the panels shown

The first solar cells manufactured were not very efficient, and did not last very long. In some cases, it took more energy to make the cells than they generated in their lifetime. Today's solar cells are much more efficient and last between 20 and 30 years. The time it takes to generate as much electricity as has been used to make the solar cells is called the **energy payback time**. The energy payback time for solar cells is between one and four years. Wind turbines do even better than this – the typical energy payback time for a wind turbine is several months.

6 a What does 'saves CO_2' mean?
b Calculate the payback time for the solar cells shown in advert C.
c Suggest why some people buy these panels.
7 Why do you think the energy payback time for wind turbines is so much less than for solar cells?

109

1 List the different presentational devices used.
2 Now complete these statements, commenting on the effect of the presentation in the science textbook. Remember to link your comment to this particular text.
   a) The writer has used the primary colours of yellow, red and blue because...
   b) The writer has used red subheadings such as 'How much money can you save by using renewable resources?' because...
   c) The writer has used a purple information panel with an exclamation mark logo because...
3 How might the same presentational devices be used differently in a leaflet persuading people to produce their own household electricity? Explain the changes you would make and the reasons why.

Presentation can also be used to communicate the writer's perspective. Look at the two posters below about climate change. **Poster A** is calling for action to fight climate change, while **Poster B** is asking whether climate change really exists. In each poster the presentational devices used help support the writer's perspective.

Poster A

Poster B

Activity 3

1 Copy and complete the table below.

a) Add any other presentational devices you can identify.

b) Then explain how the presentational devices support the perspective of the writer. One has been completed for you.

Presentational device	Invasion of the climate snatchers	Global warming?
Font style	A scratchy horror film-style font suggests how scary the writer feels climate change is.	
Font size		
Background colour		

As part of your controlled assessment task you could explore how the writers communicate their ideas and perspectives using presentation.

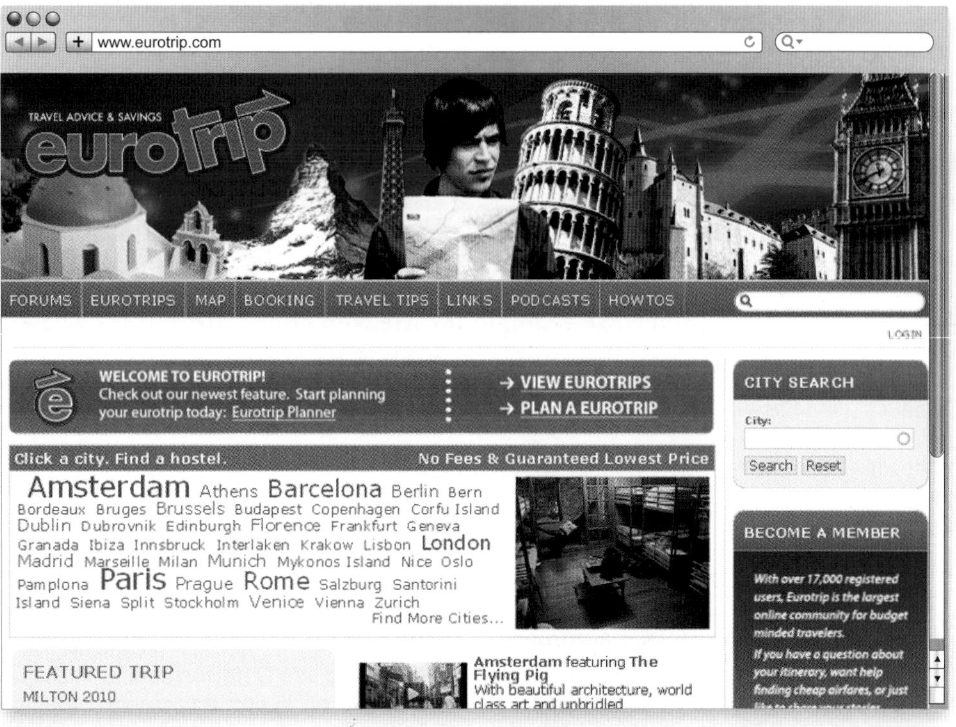

Activity 4

Write a response to this question:

How does Eurotrip use presentation to communicate their ideas and perspectives?

You should spend 10 minutes on this task.

ResultsPlus
Self assessment

Before you complete this self-assessment activity, you might like to read some sample answers to this task on the following pages (24-25).

1 Check your answer to Activity 4:

- Did you use specific examples of presentational devices in your answer?
- Did you name the presentational devices used?
- Did you comment on *how* the presentation used communicates the writer's ideas and perspectives?

2 Now try to mark your answer to Activity 4 by applying the mark scheme opposite. You will need to be careful and precise in your marking.

Band 2
- selects examples of presentational devices but does not comment on these directly
- comments on presentation are brief
- some idea of the writer's perspectives but not really linked to the example selected

Band 3
- selects appropriate examples of presentational devices to comment on and the examples chosen show some support of the points being made
- comments on presentation are sound
- includes clear exploration of the ideas and perspectives of the writer

Band 4
- selects appropriate small parts of the presentational devices to focus on in detail and the examples chosen support the points being made
- comments on presentation are detailed
- thoroughly explores the ideas and perspectives of the writer

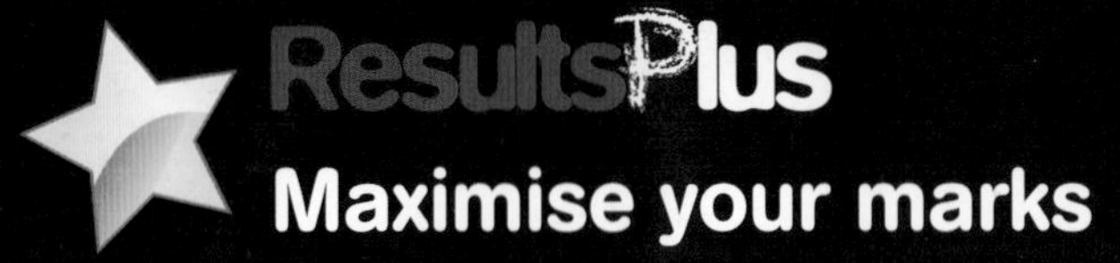

How does Eurotrip use presentation to communicate their ideas and perspectives?

Here are three student answers to the writing about presentation task on page 23. Read the answers together with the examiner comments around and after the answers. Then complete the activity at the bottom of page 25.

Student 1 – Extract typical of a grade (D) answer

Describes presentation by picking out examples.

Some understanding of the ideas connected to a clear example.

In the website Eurotrip have very clear writing and use is quite smart. For example for the web page title 'eurotrip' they have used big orange writing and this makes it stand out so you know what this page is going to be about. They have used a lot of space in between paragraphs and have used colour to make the website seem friendly and slightly informal.

Good comment on writer's perspective but not connected to a particular example.

Examiner summary

This part of the answer is typical of grade D performance. The student has selected examples from the text to demonstrate the ideas the writer is putting forward, which is shown when they comment on the colour of the packing list heading. They only do this once and the other comments lack a clear link with a particular part of the website, so the student only shows some understanding of this. If the student had commented more about friendliness and pointed to a specific part of the site they would have got a better mark.

Student 2 – Extract typical of a grade (C) answer

A clear understanding of what the writer was trying to achieve, with good links to a particular example.

The 'Eurotrip' logo gives off a friendly welcome when you enter the site. The way 'trip' is emphasised is like a plane about to fly off into the sky, linking to the idea of travel. The writer uses this because he is trying to use the logo as a sign to say "go now!" The effect on readers would be to help them know what it is about and how it will change their opinion on travelling.

Begins to consider the perspective that the writer was attempting to communicate.

Examiner summary

This part of the answer is typical of grade C performance. The student has shown clear understanding of the writer's ideas and has linked this to the example of the logo. The student shows they understand that the writer of the site is communicating on the subject of travelling abroad. They follow this up with explaining the writer's perspective and use the phrase 'go now' to show the sense of excitement the writer wanted to express. The comment on changing the reader's opinion of travel also shows understanding of the writer's perspective, but it is not expressed well enough to be given much credit.

Student 3 – Extract typical of a grade  answer

The comment on presentation and audience is developed throughout the paragraph.

Eurotrip uses bold, vivid colours which attract the younger audience. The colour blue tells us that the website is very mellow and calm, and is also for a youthful audience. As this is a website that has to be easily navigated, it is broken down into small chunks. This is also very clever because the younger audience don't want to go onto a website where there are a lot of things to read, but rather skim read through small paragraphs containing only the key points – especially if they are just trying to find information they tend to find boring.

A clear understanding of colour developed on from opening sentence well.

Continues the point that the writer has aimed the website at younger people.

Examiner summary

This part of the answer is typical of grade B performance. The student has written effectively about the use of presentation to appeal to the audience. The whole paragraph focuses on this one train of thought about what the writer was hoping to achieve. The student could have explained why a 'mellow and calm' design might also support the writer's perspective on travel.

ResultsPlus

Build better answers

Move from a Grade D to Grade C

In this part of your task you need to select a number of specific examples of presentation used by the writer. You also need to make sure you comment on how this presentation has been used. This is shown in the difference between Student 1 and Student 2. Student A's comments tended to be a description of the presentational devices or the ideas in the text but they were not connected. Student B connected the examples and the ideas much better.

Move from a Grade C to Grade B

In this part of the task you need to make sure you comment on the writer's perspective and make clear links between the examples you select and the points you are making. You need to comment in detail about the links to show you clearly understand the ideas and perspectives. Student 3 focused on a number of specific examples, but then developed one point in detail.

Putting it into Practice

1 **Explain to a partner, in as few words as possible, what a good response to presentation must include. Try to identify some key areas which you will need to develop.**

2 **Your home may contain different texts, such as newspapers and leaflets, which use presentation to help communicate their message. Write a paragraph commenting on the use of presentation to practise what you have learned and grade your response.**

7 Understanding how images are used

This lesson will help you to...

- → understand why images are used in texts
- → explore the content of images

Images can make a piece of writing look attractive or help to communicate a message much more quickly than text alone. The writer of a children's book might use an image of the events described to help the child to understand what is happening. The writer of a textbook might use an image to make information easier to understand.

Your controlled assessment task will ask you to comment on how the writers use images as presentational devices to communicate their ideas and perspectives.

Activity 1

Look at the home page of the Crimestoppers website.

1. Discuss what this page would look like without images.
2. Write down why you think the writer has included a picture of:
   a) a silhouette of a man with the words 'Most wanted'
   b) an image of the letters C and S entwined.

ResultsPlus
Watch out!

■ When writing about images, be careful not to just describe what you see. Remember to comment on *why* the image has been selected using words such as *because*, *suggests* or *implies*.

The writer's choice of image can help you to understand their perspective on the topic they are writing about. When writing about the content of an image in your task, start by **describing** what is in the picture and then **explain** why those things are included in the picture.

Activity 2

Look carefully at the image from a Crimestoppers leaflet below. Then read the description of the content of the image in the blue box.

The designer has included a city landscape because they are talking about crime and this is clearly a neighbourhood where there might be more crime. It is clearly early evening or early morning as the sun is low in the sky, this suggests...

In the foreground of the image there is a teenager looking at a mobile phone. He is wearing a hat that covers his eyes and his hood is up over his head. You cannot tell who he is. The designer has done this because...

In the background there are silhouettes of other young people, one on a bike, one wearing headphones, one wearing glasses and another hiding in an alleyway, implying that....

1. **Complete each paragraph that describes the image. You should complete the sentences, explaining why the designer has made these choices.**
2. **What does this image suggest the writer's perspective on teenagers is?**
3. **This image relies on stereotypes of young people and life in the city to make its point about crime. Do you think this is fair? Explain your answer.**
4. **What other images could the writer have used to communicate the same message? Explain your choices.**

8 Understanding the effect of images

This lesson will help you to...

→ **understand how colour, angle and composition can be used in images to create an effect on the reader**

Writers can use images to suggest ideas to a reader indirectly. Colour is the easiest way to suggest something to the reader, without telling them directly.

Colours of an image can have certain associations which the reader thinks about when he or she sees them. We make a connection between the colour red and the idea of danger without really thinking about it, for example.

Activity 1

Here are the colours on a traffic light:

1 **What do these colours suggest to the driver of a car?**

2 **If a writer used an image with these colours in it, what else could they suggest? Suggest as many ideas as you can for each colour.**

Look again at the Crimestoppers leaflet.

3 **Write a paragraph explaining how the writer has used colour. Try to use the words 'suggests' and 'implies' to explain the effects the colours create.**

The camera angle used (low, eye-level or high angle) can suggest particular ideas or perspectives. A high angle shot, for example, can be used to make something seem small or insignificant.

low angle shot

eye-level shot

high angle shot

The **composition** of the image (where people and objects are positioned) also has an effect on a reader's reactions to the ideas in the text.

Activity 2

Look at the use of angle and composition in the two images below.

1 Write a paragraph for each image, in which you:

a) describe the image and how it is composed
b) explain the use of camera angle
c) explain the effect of these features on the reader.

ResultsPlus
Self assessment

Check your answer – have you:

- selected small details from the content of the image to comment on?
- commented on the colour, angle and composition of the image?
- used the words *because*, *suggests* and *implies* to uncover the message that the image communicates?
- explained how the image can reveal the writer's point of view?

Activity 3

Look carefully at this videogame cover.

1 Discuss what ideas this image gives you about the game.

2 Write a paragraph explaining the ideas the writer communicates by using this image. Make sure that you comment on:

a) the use of colour
b) the angle used
c) the composition of the image.

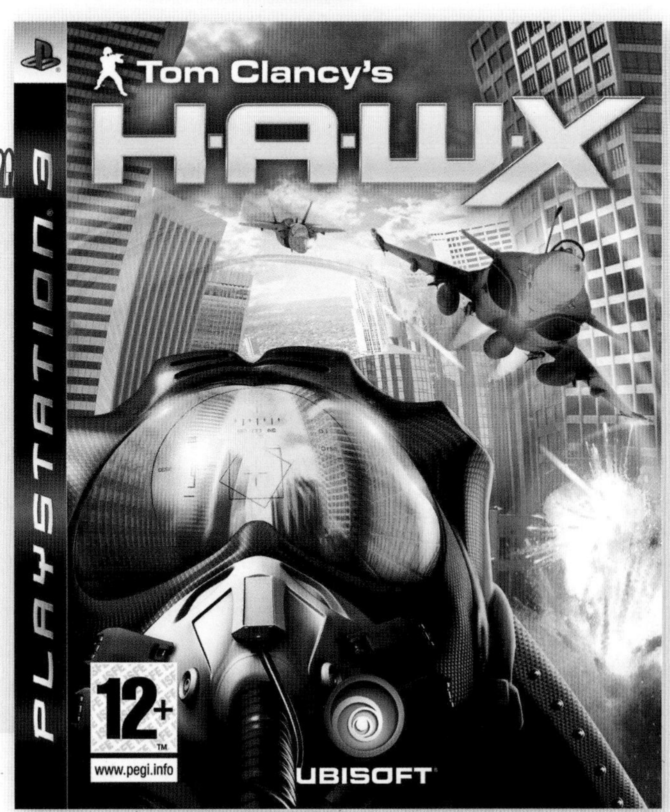

9 Understanding how moving images are used

This lesson will help you to...

- → understand why moving images are used
- → explore the impact of moving images

In your controlled assessment task you might be asked to explore the presentation choices made by a director in the production of a trailer, an advert, an extract from a documentary, an extract from a film or a pop video. Many of the choices made in a moving image are the same as for a still image, for example: colour, angles and composition. These choices can help to communicate the writer's ideas and perspectives.

Activity 1

Look at the still image from the film *Saving Private Ryan*.

1 **How are colour, angle and composition used in this shot? Make notes about each choice.**

2 **What ideas and perspectives does this image communicate? How does the writer want you to feel about war and how do the choices made help to suggest this? Write down your ideas.**

When you view moving images you need to work out what other choices have been made. Try to identify the effects of the **soundtrack** (music, dialogue, sound effects and voiceover) and **camera shots** (the way a scene was filmed).

Film directors can use different types of camera shots. For instance, they might use a **pan shot**, where they move the camera from side to side. They might also choose to **zoom in** or **zoom out**, getting closer to the action or further away from it. A **tracking shot** might be used to move alongside the action or to give the impression that the camera is part of the action.

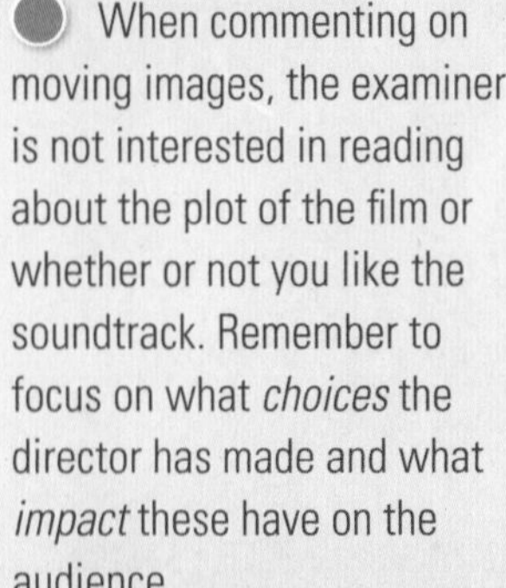

ResultsPlus
Watch out!

When commenting on moving images, the examiner is not interested in reading about the plot of the film or whether or not you like the soundtrack. Remember to focus on what *choices* the director has made and what *impact* these have on the audience.

Activity 2

Watch the trailer for *Saving Private Ryan* on the ActiveTeach.

1 **Note down the different camera shots used and what these show.**

2 **Now watch the trailer again. This time note down what you notice about the soundtrack, including the music used, what information the voiceover gives and any dialogue or sound effects.**

3 **Write a paragraph explaining what impact the director's choices have on the audience. Make sure you comment on the camera shots used as well as on the soundtrack.**

As part of your controlled assessment task you could explore how the writers use images as presentational devices to communicate their ideas and perspectives.

Activity 3

Write a response to this question:

How does Eurotrip use images to communicate their ideas and perspectives?

You should spend 10 minutes on this task.

ResultsPlus
Self assessment

Before you complete this self-assessment activity you might like to read some sample answers to this task on the following pages (32-33).

1 **Check your answer to Activity 3:**
- Did you describe the small details in the images?
- Did you explain why the designer made these choices using the word 'because'?
- Did you consider what the images might suggest or imply?
- Did you link the images used to the writer's perspective and ideas?

2 **Now try to grade your answer to Activity 3 by applying the mark scheme opposite. You will need to be careful and precise in your marking.**

Band 2
- selects images but does not comment on these directly
- comments on images are brief
- some idea of writers perspective but not really linked to the image selected

Band 3
- selects images to comment on and clearly links the examples to the points being made
- comments on images are sound and show the point being developed
- makes clear links between the images used and the writer's ideas and perspectives

Band 4
- selects small parts of the images to focus on in detail
- comments on images are detailed
- makes thorough comments on the links between the images used and the writer's ideas and perspectives of the ideas within the text

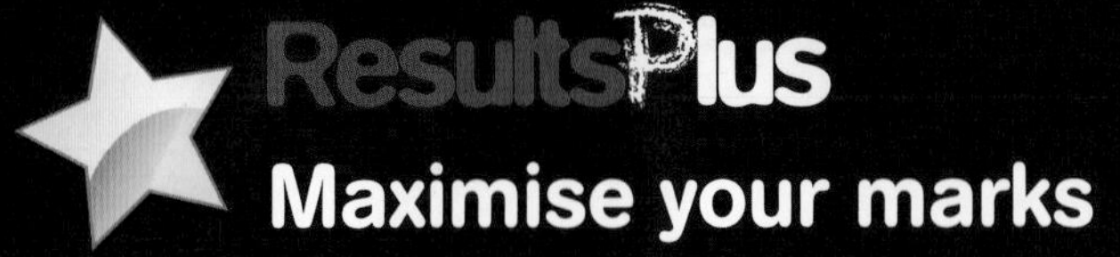

Maximise your marks

How does Eurotrip use images to communicate their ideas and perspectives?

Here are three student answers to the writing about image task on page 31. Read the answers together with the examiner comments around and after the answers. Then complete the activity at the bottom of page 33.

Student 1 – Extract typical of a grade (D) answer

Very general opening sentence that doesn't link to the image or explain why the website needs to grab your attention.

The pictures on the website are very good and grab your attention straight away. The main picture on the page is of a teenager in the middle of landmarks from Europe. This is because the website focuses on trips to Europe and there would mainly be city trips available.

An example has been selected and the next sentence begins to link it to the ideas.

The beginning of a clear response to the ideas in the text.

Examiner summary

This part of the answer is typical of grade D performance. The student has selected an image to write about and does make one comment on this image. The link between the image and the comment is clear but the student is only just beginning to develop their ideas. The student needed to make the link between the landmarks and trips to Europe clearer.

Student 2 – Extract typical of a grade (C) answer

Direct link between the image and the comment.

On Eurotrip there is a picture of a teenager in amongst a range of European landmarks. We can see that the site is aimed at young people because of the model used. We can also see that the aim of the site is to help teenagers travel around Europe because of the places around the model.

Another point made about the image.

Examiner summary

This part of the answer is typical of grade C performance. There is a clear and obvious link between the idea of the model and the landmarks and the audience and purpose of the website. The student makes two good points about the image, but neither point is developed further.

Student 2 Extract typical of a grade  answer

Direct connection between perspective in the website and the image, which is then explored more thoroughly with the use of 'therefore' to add further detail.

Eurotrip has a picture of a teenager surrounded by European landmarks. This suggests that the website can guide teenagers on their journey around Europe. The different landmarks suggest he can go to any one of these places therefore does not limit his destination to one city. The boy is looking carefully at a map to work out where to go next but he seems confident – this might be because the website has given him confidence to travel and select destinations when he is there.

A thorough comment about the idea of making the reader a confident traveller.

Examiner summary

This part of the answer is typical of grade B performance. This student has used words such as 'therefore' which show that they are adding detail to the ideas they are writing. The final sentence could have been written more confidently, removing the word 'might', but it does add further detail to the comment about the picture so it thoroughly explores the main point of the website – which is to make travellers feel safe when travelling.

ResultsPlus
Build better answers

Move from a Grade D to Grade C

In this part of your task you need to clearly comment on the links between the image and the ideas and perspectives in the website. This is shown in the difference between Student 1 and Student 2. Although these students make very similar points, Student 2 obviously connects the age of the model used to the intended audience of the website.

Move from a Grade C to Grade B

In this part of your task you need to make sure you use words such as 'therefore' and 'so' to add detail to your ideas and make clear links between the images and the ideas and perspectives of the writer. A typical B grade student would need to take very small details and explore each one thoroughly. For example, when writing about the map in the image, identify three or four things about this very small part of the image – such as we assume that the boy is a tourist; he is carefully planning his destinations; he is a confident traveller – and then link each of these points to the ideas and perspectives of the website.

Putting it into Practice

1 **Look closely at the posters on the classroom wall or from around the school. Select an image and describe it, picking out small decisions that the designer has made.**

2 **For each decision the designer has made, comment on what you think the designer was suggesting or implying about the topic being illustrated.**

10 Using language to communicate ideas and perspective

This lesson will help you to...

→ **understand how language reveals a writer's perspective**

Whatever type of text you are writing about in your controlled assessment task you need to comment on the language choices the writer has made and how these help to communicate the writer's ideas and perspective.

Activity 1

Read this extract from a BBC Radio Five Live podcast on the Ashes cricket test at Lord's.

1. **What perspective does the commentator have on the match? Do you think they are pleased that England won or unhappy that Australia was beaten? Explain your ideas.**
2. **Certain words and phrases reveal the commentator's perspective. Look at the word 'famous' – how does this reveal the commentator's perspective on the match?**
3. **Write down any other words and phrases that reveal the commentator's perspective on the match. Explain what each one shows you about the commentator's perspective.**

Well, what a famous victory that was – coming just before lunch on the fifth and final day – when Andrew Flintoff and then Graeme Swann got amongst those last five Australian wickets and saw England through to their first victory here at Lord's in 75 years. It was Flintoff who led the way – man of the match – who bowled at blistering pace – unchanged from the Pavilion End – he took his first five-wicket haul here and what a way to bow out from this famous old ground.

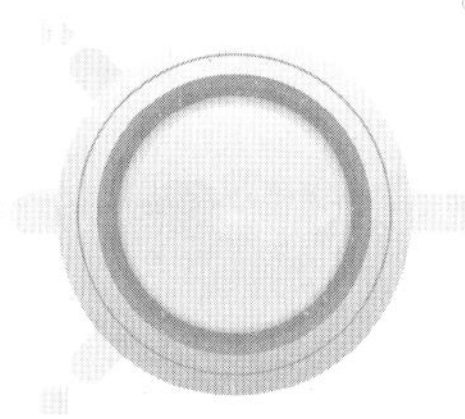

ResultsPlus
Controlled assessment tip

Being able to use the correct term to describe the language used will make your answer sound more confident. However, if you don't know words like alliteration, you can still describe the language used by saying the writer repeats a certain consonant in their writing, for example.

Activity 2

Now read the extract opposite from an online news article from the *New Zealand Herald*. The writer is reporting the same victory by England. However, the writer's perspective is different and this affects the way they write about the match.

1. **How is this writer's perspective different from the commentator's perspective in the Five Live podcast? Discuss your ideas.**
2. **Pick out words and phrases that communicate the perspective of the writer in the online news article.**
3. **Write a paragraph explaining how the language choices differ between the podcast and the online news article.**

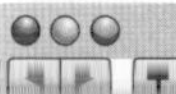

LONDON - Australia's 75-year unbeaten test run at Lord's is over.

From Tom Wald in London, England July 20, 2009

After Michael Clarke (136) and Brad Haddin (80) had revived Australia's hopes of pulling off an incredible victory, Flintoff quickly slapped them down by taking 3-43 in an unforgettable ten-over spell from the Pavilion End on Monday.

Mitchell Johnson (63) played an aggressive hand but didn't have the necessary support and was the last man to go, bowled by spinner Graeme Swann (4-87).

Australian skipper Ricky Ponting said his men were hurting. 'We have had a very proud record here over a number of years now and it is obviously disappointing to lose any test match,' he said.

To comment effectively on how language communicates a writer's perspective, you need to be able to identify the specific language techniques the writer uses.

Activity 3

Look at the extract from manchesterunited-blog.com. The writer of this text is a fan of Manchester United and the language he chooses shows this.

1 **What ideas does the writer communicate in this blog posting? What is the writer's perspective on the signing of Michael Owen?**

2 **The writer uses the following language techniques in the blog.**

- Questions
- Superlatives
- Repetition
- Slang
- Exaggeration
- List

For each technique, select an example from the blog and comment on how it communicates the writer's ideas and perspective.

www.manchesterunited-blog.com

HOME ABOUT ADVERTISE CONTACT NETWORK SUBSCRIBE TO FEED SUBSCRIBE BY EMAIL

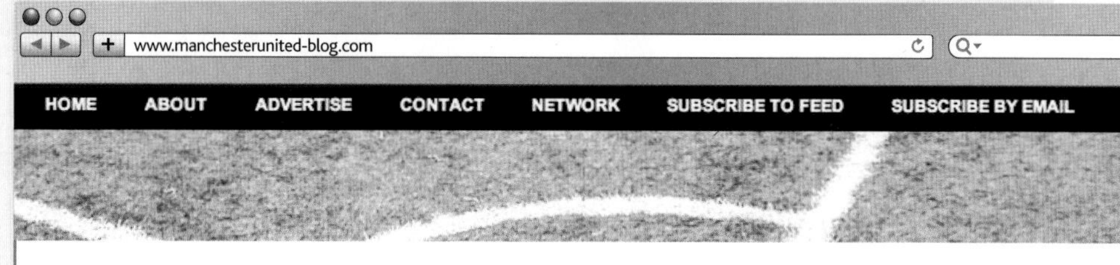

Owen gets legendary number 7. Potential for a legendary striker partnership with Rooney wearing number 10?

Posted July 14th, 2009 by Franky in History, Squad, Why MU is the Greatest

When earlier today the news was announced that Michael Owen [is to wear] the legendary Manchester United number 7, previously worn by ManUtd legends Bryan Robson, Eric Cantona, David Beckham and Cristiano Ronaldo, I shuddered. Was one of our most traditional and important numbers in the history of Old Trafford going to an ex-Liverpool player?

But quickly I remembered that this was a sign of Alex Ferguson's confidence in Owen, just like he handed the number 7 to Ronaldo straight upon arrival. The gaffer obviously has mellowed, even though we all know that he still wants Man Utd to win most League titles in history, more than Liverpool FC.

Two seasons ago Wayne Rooney was handed another legendary ManUtd number 10, Denis Law's favourite number. Does this partnership have the potential to become a legendary one? The #7 and #10 partnership, the most feared striker tandem for every defence in England and Europe?

11 Exploring the impact of language choices

This lesson will help you to...

→ **understand the impact language choices can have on the reader**

Writers make language choices in order to create a particular effect on the reader. For example, writers know that:

- questions will encourage readers to consider the answer
- repetition will make an idea seem more important
- exaggeration will ensure the reader believes that there must be some truth in what is being said if the writer is so passionate.

Activity 1

Look at the text below from the DirectGov website.

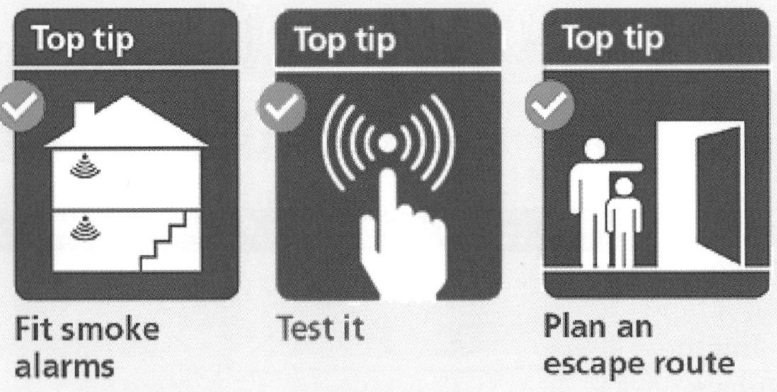

1. **What is the purpose of this text?**
2. **What impact does putting the imperative, the command word, at the beginning of each sentence have on the reader?**
3. **Write a sentence explaining how the language choice helps the text to achieve its purpose. Think about what the impact of the text would be if different language was used, for example: 'You could test it'.**

The writer can also use language that will appeal to the reader's thoughts or emotions.

Activity 2

Watch the 'Ash 2008' video on the ActiveTeach, it is taken from the Fire Kills section of the direct.gov.uk website.

1. Pick out the language choices made to appeal to the reader and identify the techniques used.
2. Explain the impact that each language choice might have on the reader.
3. What idea does the writer want to communicate in this video? How do their language choices help them to communicate this?

Activity 3

Look at the leaflet from the Children's Burns Trust.

1. What ideas and perspective is the writer communicating?
2. What language techniques has the writer used?
3. What impact does the writer hope these language techniques will have?
4. How does the language the writer has chosen help to communicate their ideas and perspective?

12 Commenting on language choices

This lesson will help you to...

→ **comment effectively on how language communicates ideas and perspectives**

To be able to comment effectively on how language communicates ideas and perspectives in your response to your controlled assessment task, you need to:

- look carefully at specific examples
- identify the techniques used
- explain why the writer has used each technique
- explore the impact it will have on the reader, listener or viewer.

Activity 1

Read this extract from a blog by Kit Whitfield.

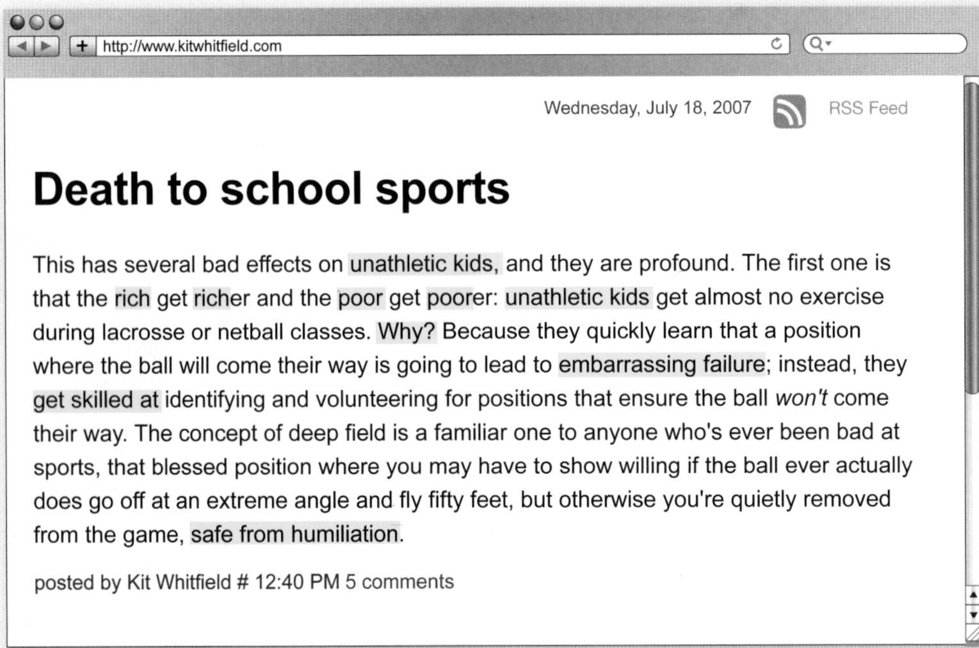

http://www.kitwhitfield.com

Wednesday, July 18, 2007 RSS Feed

Death to school sports

This has several bad effects on unathletic kids, and they are profound. The first one is that the rich get richer and the poor get poorer: unathletic kids get almost no exercise during lacrosse or netball classes. Why? Because they quickly learn that a position where the ball will come their way is going to lead to embarrassing failure; instead, they get skilled at identifying and volunteering for positions that ensure the ball *won't* come their way. The concept of deep field is a familiar one to anyone who's ever been bad at sports, that blessed position where you may have to show willing if the ball ever actually does go off at an extreme angle and fly fifty feet, but otherwise you're quietly removed from the game, safe from humiliation.

posted by Kit Whitfield # 12:40 PM 5 comments

1 Summarise the ideas in this blog.

2 The writer has used a number of techniques in this article. Including:

- emotive language
- questions
- slang
- repetition

Examples of these have been highlighted in the text. Write down each technique and match it to the example.

3 Kit Whitfield has used exaggeration in her blog to make a point. Identify where she could be said to be exaggerating. What does the writer hope to achieve by using over-the-top language like this?

To be able to comment on language choice only takes a small amount of text. You do not need to comment on all the language used by the writer. It is important to select the best example to comment on.

Activity 2

Look at this poster for innocent smoothies:

1 **Here are some quotations from the text. Select one quotation that you think is perfect for exploring the language used by the writer:**

   "We crush all of this... into this."

   "nothing but nothing but fruit."

   "it's a tight fit like spandex trousers"

   "Not just the liquidy bit (also known as juice) but the whole darned shooting match"

2 **Identify the language used by the writer in the quotation you have selected. You might find some of the following techniques useful:**
   - humour
   - personal pronouns
   - brackets
   - ellipses
   - repetition
   - incomplete sentences
   - made up words

3 **Explain why you selected your quotation. How does it help you to explain how the writer uses language in the text?**

To comment effectively on language you first need to work out the ideas and perspective in the text and then build a paragraph explaining how the language used helps to communicate these ideas and perspectives.

Activity 3

The shoe is dead.
Long live the muscle-toning, posture-improving, calorie-burning, joint-protecting, back-relieving multilateral system that you happen to wear on your feet.
If they weren't so radically different, if their only purpose was to look good with jeans, if they only protected your feet instead of your entire body, we might have been able to find a simpler word for them. Something like shoes.

Style: Nama. theantishoe.com

MBT
The anti-shoe.

Read the advertisement for MBT shoes.

1 Use some of the strategies you have practised earlier in this unit to work out the ideas and perspective of the writer.

2 Identify examples of the following language techniques in the text:

- list
- compounds
- incomplete sentences
- technical vocabulary
- personal pronouns
- repetition

3 Copy and complete the following table. For each example, comment on:

a) how the language has been used and what impact it has on the reader

b) how the language technique influences the reader's understanding of the ideas and the perspective the writer is communicating.

Example	Language technique used	How the term has been used/impact on the reader	How this influences the reader's understanding of the writers. ideas and perspective

By working through the text in this way you have collected all the information you need to be able to write the part of your controlled assessment task exploring how the language communicates the writer's ideas and perspective.

Activity 4

1 Using one row from your table from Activity 3, write a paragraph on the language used in the advertisement. Remember to use the words 'suggests', 'because', or 'implies' in your paragraph.

As part of this question you could explore how the writers communicate their ideas and perspectives using language.

Activity 5

Write a response to this question:

How does Eurotrip use language to communicate their ideas and perspectives?

You should spend 10 minutes on this task.

ResultsPlus Self assessment

Before you complete this self-assessment activity, you might like to read some sample answers to this task on the following pages (42-43).

1. **Check your answer to Activity 5:**
   - Did you select quotations from the text?
   - Did you describe the language chosen by the writer using technical terms?
   - Did you consider what might be *suggested* or *implied* by the language choices made by the writer?
   - Did you explain how the language reveals the writer's ideas and perspectives?

2. **Now try to grade your answer to Activity 5 by applying the mark scheme opposite. You will need to be careful and precise in your marking.**

Band 2
- selects quotations to comment on and begins to link the examples to the points being made
- comments on language are brief
- some idea of the writer's perspective but not really linked to language used

Band 3
- selects quotations to comment on and clearly links the examples to the points being made
- comments on language are sound and show the point being developed
- makes clear links between the language used and the writer's ideas and perspectives

Band 4
- selects small parts of the quotations (perhaps one word or a sentence) to focus on in detail
- comments on language are detailed
- makes thorough comments on the links between the language used and the writer's ideas and perspectives

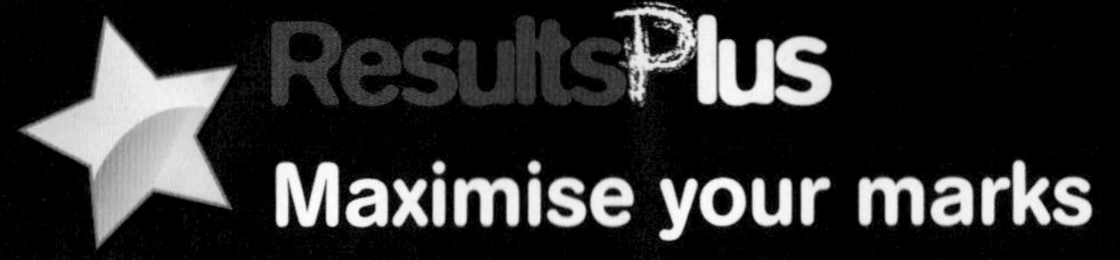

How does Eurotrip use language to communicate their ideas and perspectives?

Here are three student answers to the writing about language task on page 41. Read the answers together with the examiner comments around and after the answers. Then complete the activity at the bottom of page 43.

Student 1 – Extract typical of a grade (D) answer

The writer uses 'you' a lot in Eurotrip and mentions that a lot of people use the site. They also use imperatives to tell the reader what to do when they use words like 'click'. The site is trying to make people feel that they can trust them and that they will help them.

Quotations have been used.

Mostly descriptive but this last sentence begins to link the language choices to the writer's perspective.

Examiner summary

This part of the answer is typical of grade D performance. This student has selected quotations and makes a good attempt at identifying the language chosen. There is a suggested link between the comment about wanting to trust the site and the use of imperatives and 'you', but it is not clearly made. The student could have used the word 'because' to show the connection between the language and the comment.

Student 2 – Extract typical of a grade (C) answer

Clear description of the language used followed by a quotation to support the idea.

A clear comment on the language chosen.

Eurotrip uses statistics as it says "with over 17,000 registered users, eurotrip forum is the largest community on the internet for budget minded travellers backpacking in Europe" this shows to the reader that it is a well used website and that it is not a con. Europtrip also uses personal pronouns saying "tips to help you plan for what's to come" which makes the reader feel welcome.

Another description of the language chosen and a comment on the writer's perspective.

Examiner summary

This part of the answer is typical of grade C performance. This student has clearly described statistics and personal pronouns and selected an appropriate quotation. They have also made a clear comment on this example, saying something about the ideas in the site. The quotation for the statistics is too long and the student could have linked the use of statistics and personal pronoun to show they can explore the ideas and perspectives thoroughly.

Student 3 Extract typical of a grade B answer

Eurotrip uses some factual language when it says "With over 17,000 registered users" and this makes the reader realise that it's a good site if so many people use it, people want to be part of a large group. The site also uses instructive language when it uses the command "Click here for free shipping." – the imperative "click" clearly tells the reader what to do. This is because the site aims to appear helpful and caring, shown when it says "This is a great tool that helps you choose the rail pass that's right for you." The use of the personal pronoun "you" means the reader feels like the site cares for their needs individually.

Some detail to support the comment on why the website mentioned the number of users.

The quotation selected is the appropriate part of the text that the student then comments on.

The comment on the imperative and personal pronoun are connected to one point in the text, showing a thorough exploration of the ideas and perspectives.

Examiner summary

This part of the answer is typical of grade B performance. This student selects the appropriate part of a sentence to explore factual language and its use. The addition of the idea about the audience wanting to feel like a large group is detailed. The student's response is particularly strong when it connects the imperative and the personal pronoun and thoroughly explores the idea of the reader needing to feel cared for.

ResultsPlus

Build better answers

Move from a Grade D to Grade C

In this part of your task you need to clearly identify the language chosen by the writer and then comment on how this reflects the ideas and perspectives in the text. This is shown in the difference between Student 1 and Student 2, as Student 1 doesn't clearly link the language selected to the comment they make about the website.

Move from a Grade C to Grade B

In this part of your task you need to make sure that you select quotations, identify the language used and then comment on that language choice. Students working at a B grade typically comment about the different language selected to form an overall view of the writer's perspective – which in the case of Eurotrip is to reassure the reader that they will be looked after if they use this website.

Putting it into Practice

1 **Choose one page from a school text book. Write as many statements as you can in which you describe the language used. You could use the following to help you:**

The writer has used . . . when they write ". . .".

2 **For three of the statements you have written add the word "because" and complete the statement explaining how the language has been used. So, your statement would begin:**

The writer has used . . . when they write ". . ." because . . . .

13 Selecting appropriate examples

This lesson will help you to...

→ select appropriate examples from a text

→ use examples to help support a detailed response

When selecting examples from the texts in your controlled assessment task it is important to remind yourself of:

- the ideas
- the perspective
- the audience
- the purpose.

You then need to find examples of image, presentation and language that are used to help the text be effective.

Activity 1

Read this blog from *Empire* magazine written by the journalist Chris Hewitt.

1 What ideas do Chris Hewitt communicate?

2 What is Chris Hewitt's perspective on ten Oscar nominees?

3 Who is the intended reader of the blog?

4 What is its purpose?

http://www.empireonline.com/empireblog/

10 Oscar Nominees Per Year?

posted on Thursday June 25, 2009, 09:58 by Chris Hewitt

So, as of next year, the Oscars' Best Picture race will include ten nominees, rather than the traditional five, the biggest sea change for the ceremony since the minting of the Best Animated Feature Film category (ironically, a category that may be threatened by this new move; more on that later). It's a decision that has split pundits down the middle. Everyone's favourite grumpy old man, Jeff Wells over at Hollywood Elsewhere, has bah-humbugged the whole enterprise – "Why didn't the Academy decide to nominate 15 films for Best Picture?" he asks – while Steven Zeitchick at The Hollywood Reporter thinks it's a potentially positive move, calling it a "shrewd marketing move" even if it's also "a questionable policy change." Meanwhile, in my initial spur-of-the-moment reaction in our news story, I pooh-poohed the idea, seeing it as a largely cynical move to acknowledge films that don't have a chance of scooping the big prize. And I still stand by that – largely. It's pretty apparent that the Academy decided to do this, not to return the Oscars to their heyday (the last time more than five films completed for the li'l golden guy was in 1943, back when Hitler had no idea that he would become a YouTube punchline), but because of the criticism that came its way in the wake of the shocking snub handed out to the likes of **The Dark Knight, Gran Torino, Wall-E** and **Eagle Eye**, four films which were demonstrably better than actual Best Picture nominee, **The Reader**.

Empire Blog RSS Feed

CATEGORIES

- London Film Festival 2009
- Words From The Wise
- The Empire Blog
- Comic-Con Diaries

RECENT POSTS

- Finally! Demos's LFF round-up... By Damon Wise
- Help Avert World War III By Helen O'Hara
- How Scary Should Kids Movies Be? By Helen O'Hara
- Videobiogisode Day 16 By Chris Hewitt
- Who Should Host The Oscars Now? By Helen O'Hara
- Videobiogisode Day 15 By Chris Hewitt
- Videobiogisode Day 14 By Chris Hewitt
- Videobiogisode Day 13 By Chris Hewitt

ResultsPlus
Controlled assessment tip

Selecting just a word or a short phrase to quote when writing about language is often more effective than writing out the whole sentence. Try to keep quotations as brief as possible, selecting only the part that is relevant to the point you are making.

You have now collected your initial comments in response to Chris Hewitt's blog. Next you need to show how the writer's use of image, presentation and language supports your comments.

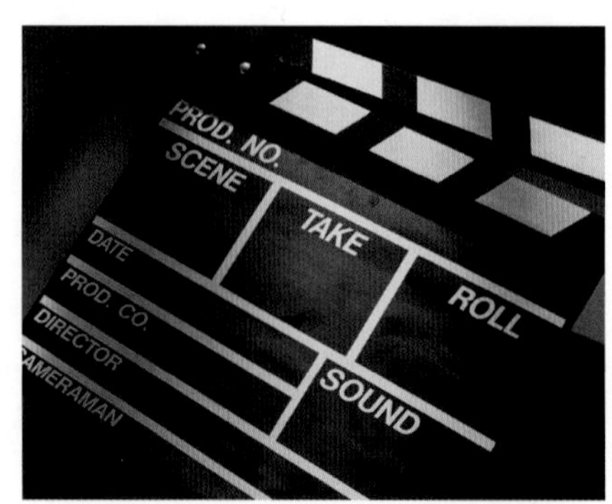

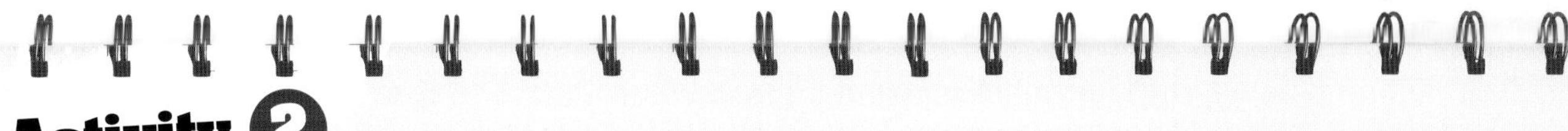

Activity 2

1 Find examples of each of the following features that have been used by the writer of the blog:

- bold text
- blue font
- larger font
- use of slang
- use of an incomplete sentence.

2 What other language, presentation or image features used in the blog can you identify?

3 Select the examples that will help you to talk about the audience, purpose, ideas and perspectives of the blog.

4 Explain your choice of examples. You could copy and complete the following table to help you do this.

Idea	Example of image, presentation or language that supports your idea	How does the example you have selected support the idea you had about the text?

To build a successful response you need to build these examples into a paragraph. For example:

The blog contains bold lettering for the films such as 'The Dark Knight' and 'Gran Torino'. These stand out in the text and may draw in readers who have an interest in these films.

Activity 3

Look back at your table from the previous activity.

1 Take the information you have put in one row of the table and write it out in full sentences. Use the order of the columns to order your sentences in the paragraph.

14 Comparing how writers use presentation and language

This lesson will help you to...

- → use vocabulary that will help you compare
- → make appropriate comparisons between writers' use of presentation and language

In the controlled assessment task you will have to compare two different texts to show how writers use presentation and language to communicate their ideas and perspectives. The two texts will be on a similar theme, so you need to be able to:

- identify what ideas and perspective the writers are trying to communicate.
- compare the ways both writers use image, presentation and language to communicate these ideas and perspectives.

Activity 1

The ideas in a text will be adapted for the different audiences who will read the text. Look at the front cover of NME and the website www.ilikemusic.co.uk. Both texts focus on music but appeal to different audiences.

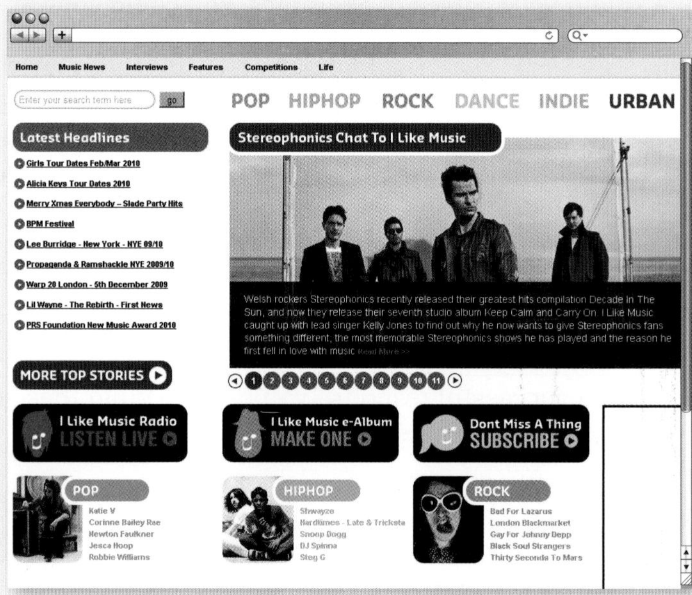

1 Who do you think the audience is for each text? Discuss your ideas.

2 Copy and complete this table. Note down any details from the two texts that helped you to identify the audience of the text. Some text has been completed for you.

	NME	I Like Music
presentation and images		*Use of brightly coloured boxes.*
language	*"Album verdict – glitter or gutter?"*	

3 Select one example that has been identified. Explain how this part of the text helped you to identify the audience.

You are also expected to comment on the perspective the texts give on music.

Activity 2

Podcasts do not have images to help communicate the perspective of the writer. Instead they use presentational devices such as music and sound effects to present their ideas. There is also more emphasis on the language that the speaker uses.

Listen to the first 2.13mins of the Channel 4 radio podcast on the ActiveTeach.

1 Copy and complete this table. Explain how the choices made by the writer give the reader a particular perspective of music.

Example	Perspective on music
Music – the opening chaotic sounding guitar solo	
Language – "In the heart of the dirty depths of east London"	
Language – "everyone's chilling and it's kinda cool and under control"	
Sound effect – the mechanical sounding voice for "4Radio"	

When you are comparing two texts in your controlled assessment task you need to look at presentation and language in turn and explore the similarities and differences in the way each writer has used these. It is not enough to write about each text on its own – you need to use connectives to make your comparisons clear.

Activity 3

Look again at the three texts that focus on music from Activities 1 and 2. Using the connectives below:

- similarly
- yet
- and
- also
- on the other hand
- whereas
- however
- but
- both

1 Write a statement comparing the use of image in two of the texts.

2 Write a statement comparing the use of presentation in two of the texts.

3 Write a statement comparing the use of language in two of the texts.

Activity 4

1 Write a paragraph about two of the texts. Compare their use of image, presentation or language. Link the comparison to the perspective that the text has on music.

ResultsPlus
Build better answers

Look at this part of a controlled assessment task: **Your task is to compare the material on two texts.**

■ A Band 2 answer will include **some comparisons** but these might only appear at the beginning of paragraphs or in a conclusion at the end.

● A Band 3 answer will have **sound comparisons** of image, presentation and language throughout the answer. However, it may deal with each text separately.

▲ A Band 4 answer will include **specific and detailed comparisons** of the two texts, with detailed comments on image, presentation and language throughout the answer. The selection of examples included will be detailed and appropriate, and will support the points being made.

Controlled Assessment Practice

Examiner's tip

This is a sample Unit 1 controlled assessment for GCSE English and GCSE English Language.

Examiner's tip

Your controlled assessment task will be based on a theme. All the questions and texts will focus on that theme.

Examiner's tip

These are the texts provided by Edexcel. You must pick two of these texts.

Turn to page 50 to see two of these texts.

Guidance for students: Reading/Studying Written Language (Reading) Task

What do I have to do?
You will complete one reading/studying written language (reading) task on the theme of the environment.

You must complete this task on your own.

How much time do I have?
Following your preparation, you will have up to two hours to complete the task.

How do I prepare for the task?
For the chosen theme:

- select two texts from the Edexcel texts provided
- prepare by making notes and planning your response to the task.

Environment texts

1 *Guardian* podcast	2 Aeroplanes and Global Warming article
3 Greenpeace Climate Change webpage*	4 Your Environment magazine cover
5 The Great Global Warming Swindle trailer	6 *The Times* article on air travel*

What must my response to the task show?
The response must show that you can:

- make comparisons between two environment texts
- select appropriate details from two environment texts to support your ideas
- explore how writers use presentation and language to communicate their ideas and perspectives in two environment texts.

How should I present my response?
A written response of up to 1000 words.

The Reading/Studying Written Language (Reading) Task for the student

Your task is to compare the material from two texts on the environment.

In your comparison you must:

- explore how the writers communicate their ideas and perspectives
- comment on how the writers use presentation and language
- include examples to illustrate the points you make.

Examiner's tip

Be sure your response covers these points!

Here are two of the texts provided for this task:

'You don't need to forsake your fun in the sun to help combat climate change.' Jane Knight. *The Times*. 17 November 2007

You don't need to forsake your fun in the sun to help combat climate change

Going green isn't just about the number of flights you make, it's also the type of holiday you choose and how you behave on it.

Jane Knight: *Deputy Travel Editor*

What's to be done? In the week that the UN Secretary General Ban Ki Moon visited Antarctica to be told that an ice sheet covering a fifth of the continent may crumble, we also hear that more travellers are balking at spending extra on holidays to help curb climate change.

And who can blame them? If dinner-table chatter is anything to go by, my friends are sick of hearing that they should forsake their fun in the sun to reduce their carbon footprint. No one wants to feel guilty about taking those well-earned holidays. And why should they, asks a colleague pointedly, when livestock generates more harmful emissions through – er – excessive flatulence than aircraft do?

Already faced with hefty fuel surcharges, passengers are reluctant to shell out more, even if it does help the environment. A study by the travel industry marketing specialist BLM Media showed that 35 per cent of respondents would not pay an extra £20 a holiday to offset carbon emissions, while an even greater 59 per cent would not cut down on the number of times they go abroad. Which is why Qatar Airways' announcement this week that it aims to be the first airline to be powered by a gas-based fuel could be revolutionary. It may not happen – an in-depth study is first needed – but at least this shows that airlines are doing something more than passing the green buck on to passengers. Virgin Atlantic has already announced plans to run a plane on biofuel next year.

Going green, though, isn't just about cutting the number of flights you make or offsetting your carbon emissions. It's also about the type of holiday you choose and how you behave on it. I've lost count of the number of hotels that trumpet their "green" credentials by encouraging you to recycle your bath towels, then change your towels twice daily anyway. I prefer to stay in small lodges or hotels where locals form part of the workforce and where hoteliers become involved in the local community, the kind of place you'll find on the useful website responsibletravel.com.

Eco-tourism doesn't have to be the oxymoron that the wildlife advocate Richard Leakey says it is. But as he points out in this issue, it does need international standards. We know how environmentally friendly washing machines are when we buy them, so why can't tourism be rated in a similar way?

Above all, responsible tourism is about awareness, not necessarily at increased cost. Ten years ago, recycling your rubbish in England was almost unheard of. What we need today is a similar change in attitude towards how we holiday.

The message is starting to trickle through. Just minutes after the New Forest this week took three accolades in the Virgin Holidays Responsible Tourism Awards, organised by Responsibletravel.com, Jamaica's tourism chiefs invited the man behind it all to their country, so they could benefit from his wisdom. Responsible tourism doesn't have to cost more, and it doesn't mean we have to stop travelling, but if we want our children, and our children's children, to benefit from travel as we do, we need to start thinking in a slightly deeper shade of green.

Climate Change Webpage
Greenpeace UK

Unit 1 English Today: Writing

This section of the book will help you to develop your writing skills, exploring how to write for different audiences and purposes, and to express your ideas clearly and precisely. The texts and activities in this unit will help you develop the skills you need to generate ideas for your writing task, plan it effectively and to structure and craft your writing by using engaging vocabulary and sentences, all of which will help you to achieve the best grade that you can in your Unit 1 controlled assessment task

Your assessment

This unit is a controlled assessment unit. You will complete one writing task which you will have two hours to complete. You can write up to 1000 words. You will be asked to complete one task from a choice of two, which will be linked to the theme of your reading task in this unit. You will have had the chance to look at the task and make notes to plan your response in advance so that you feel prepared to complete this part of the controlled assessment.

Your response to the task must show that you can:

- ✔ make choices in your writing that are appropriate to the audience and purpose
- ✔ make sure that you spell, punctuate and use grammar accurately and appropriately for the purpose of your writing and to achieve the desired effect.

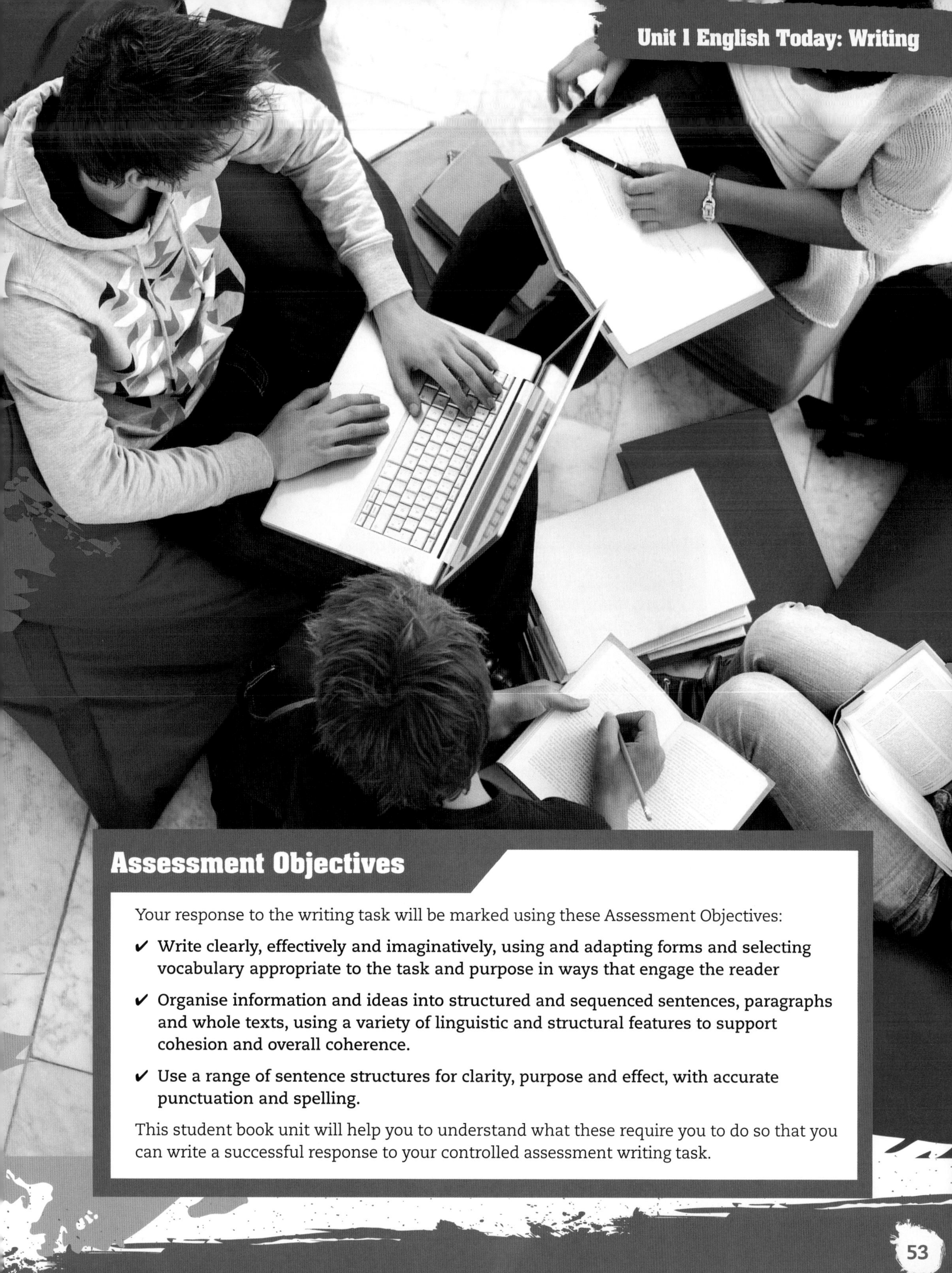

Assessment Objectives

Your response to the writing task will be marked using these Assessment Objectives:

- ✔ Write clearly, effectively and imaginatively, using and adapting forms and selecting vocabulary appropriate to the task and purpose in ways that engage the reader
- ✔ Organise information and ideas into structured and sequenced sentences, paragraphs and whole texts, using a variety of linguistic and structural features to support cohesion and overall coherence.
- ✔ Use a range of sentence structures for clarity, purpose and effect, with accurate punctuation and spelling.

This student book unit will help you to understand what these require you to do so that you can write a successful response to your controlled assessment writing task.

1 Purpose

This lesson will help you to...

- → identify and understand a range of purposes
- → understand how to write for different purposes

Your controlled assessment writing task will ask you to write for a particular purpose. There are many different purposes for writing, including providing information, persuading people, explaining something, arguing a point of view, commenting on a topic and reviewing an event or product. The purpose of a text will affect what content is included.

Text A: Review

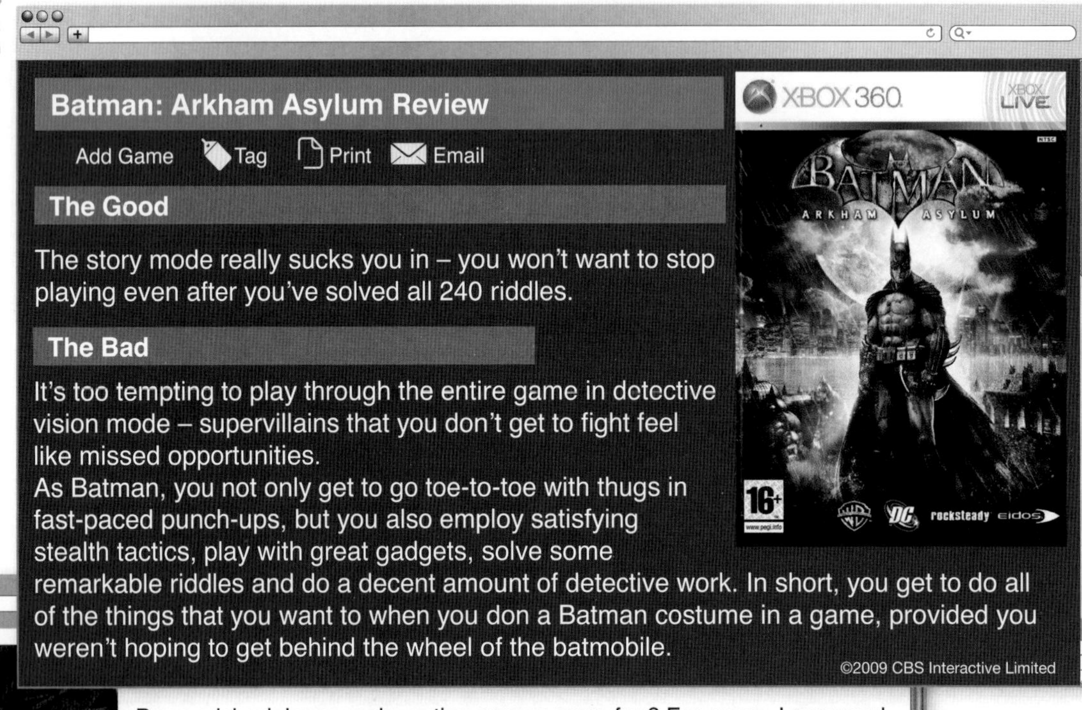

Batman: Arkham Asylum Review

Add Game Tag Print Email

The Good

The story mode really sucks you in – you won't want to stop playing even after you've solved all 240 riddles.

The Bad

It's too tempting to play through the entire game in detective vision mode – supervillains that you don't get to fight feel like missed opportunities.

As Batman, you not only get to go toe-to-toe with thugs in fast-paced punch-ups, but you also employ satisfying stealth tactics, play with great gadgets, solve some remarkable riddles and do a decent amount of detective work. In short, you get to do all of the things that you want to when you don a Batman costume in a game, provided you weren't hoping to get behind the wheel of the batmobile.

Text B: Argue

Does grisly violence make action games more fun? For years, I assumed the free market had answered that question with a resounding 'yes'.

If shoot-'em-up games were insanely gory, it was, I figured, because developers were simply giving their hardcore young-dude audience what it wanted. Violence sells because violence works: it's crucial to creating a sense of dastardly fun. Right?

Maybe not. In fact, some recent and fascinating scientific work suggests precisely the opposite: in a paper in January's *Personality and Social Psychology Bulletin*, a group of researchers found that violence might be the least compelling part of our favorite videogames.

Activity 1

1 Read Texts A and B above, which are both about computer games. Spot three differences in the type of information that is included in the two texts. For example:

Text A includes details about one game whereas Text B talks about a type of game.

2 Select a computer game or television programme you know well. Write two sentences for a **review** of this game or programme using similar details to those included in Text A.

3 Now consider your own opinion about videogame violence. Write a paragraph for an article **arguing** your point of view.

4 What words are used in the review text (Text A) to show the writer's opinions and feelings? For example: *Satisfying*

5 Identify the language techniques used in the argument text (Text B) to express the writer's point of view. For example: *The first line is a question*

Activity 2

1 Read the three short extracts from texts with different purposes, below. Identify the language techniques used in each text to help achieve its purpose. The first example has been completed for you.

2 Write three short paragraphs that inform, persuade and explain the computer game or television programme that you wrote about in Activity 1.

Inform
A videogame console is an interactive entertainment computer or electronic device that produces a video display signal which can be used with a display device (a television, monitor, etc.) to display a videogame.

Technical terms

Lots of nouns and verbs

Facts

Persuade
Nintendo changes the way you play by maximising the fun and minimising the fuss. The Wii console makes you feel less like a player and more like you're in the game

Explain
Why do we play videogames? The need for play is a primary component of human development and has been with us since the dawn of intelligence. Even in the less sophisticated brains of animals can be seen the impetus that leads to play. So before we tackle videogaming, we should assess why we, as a species, need playtime so strongly.

As part of your preparation for your controlled assessment task, it will be helpful to find a text that has a similar purpose (and, ideally, a similar subject) to the one that you are going to write. This will help you to understand what decisions you should make about what to include and how to write.

Activity 3

1 Find a text that has a similar purpose to the one that you are being asked to write.

2 Annotate a copy of the text with notes about the decisions that the writer has made about what to write about and how to write.

3 Make a list of the techniques that you use in your response, based on the ones that you have identified in the text that you found.

2 Audience

This lesson will help you to...

→ understand how to write for different audiences

As well as giving you a purpose, the controlled assessment writing task will tell you the audience you are writing for. Different readers need and expect different things from a text.

Making choices about how to write for an audience means we have to make **generalisations**. Part of writing for an audience is knowing what they would be interested in reading about. We need to assume that most people in a certain group would act in a certain way or like certain things, such as sci-fi fans liking aliens.

In your controlled assessment task you will need to select words or phrases that are appropriate for your audience **register**: for example, simple sentences for children or technical words for experts. Think about the amount of technical detail they can cope with, and how lively or humorous your text would need to be to keep their attention.

ResultsPlus
Build better answers

Look at this controlled assessment task:
Write a letter to parents informing them of some of the after school activities run by your school.

■ A Band 2 answer will show **some grasp of audience**, for example by referring to them or addressing them in an appropriate way.

● A Band 3 answer will have a **clear sense of audience** throughout the writing, with the level of formality being largely appropriate for the audience. For parents this would mean writing formally so that the letter sounds professional.

▲ A Band 4 answer will sustain this sense of formality throughout and will also **select the right tone for the audience**, whether this be amusing, serious, confrontational, etc.

Activity 1

Look at the texts below on Formula One racing (**Texts A and B**), which are aimed at different audiences.

Text A

Technical Taku tries to use his latest onboard telemetry to overtake his friends during the race. It is not until he gets a call from Franco that his high-tech superpowers are fully activated. A flashing dashboard, raised airbox and elevated sidepods are sure signs that Taku has engaged his 'super-gadget' mode. Which gadget will he use this time to help Franco and his friends? X-Ray Vision? Extending skis?

Annotations: Use of a character (Taku); Exciting adjectives (flashing); Quick-fire questions (X-Ray Vision? Extending skis?)

Text B

Hamilton was signed to the young driver programme in 1998 after McLaren's Ron Dennis observed his rapid ascent through the racing ranks. Hamilton possessed undeniable prodigious talent and he began racking up karting titles and building up an impressive array of trophies almost from the moment he started racing.

Annotations: Factual (Hamilton was signed to the young driver programme in 1998); Naming without explanation (McLaren's); Praise (possessed undeniable prodigious talent)

1 Use the highlighted features to identify who you think the audience is for each text.

2 As a writer, what language choices would you make for the following audiences?

a) mechanics who know a lot about cars
b) young females watching Formula One for the first time.

Activity 2

Read the texts below from an entry on a web forum (**Text C**) and from a newspaper article in *The Guardian* (**Text D**).

Text C

Hey gents and ladies ... have you heard? Michael Schumacher has confirmed that he would consider coming back from retirement if Ferrari asked him to. We all know that Ferrari will ask him to, so I'd say I'll get my wish at last. To watch two of my favourite drivers go at it one on one, it's a dream come true really. You know how Michael is like... he's going to want to start stirring things up (that's my Mikey for you!!).

Text D

Murray Walker is to be part of the BBC Formula One commentary team next year – but only on the web.

Walker, whose excitable commentary style and on-air bloopers made him synonymous with F1 coverage on television, moved from the BBC to ITV when the commercial broadcaster took over live coverage more than a decade ago.

1. Identify the language features used to create an informal register in Text C.
2. What language features are used in Text D to create a formal register?
3. Imagine you have been asked to report the same rumour about Michael Schumacher in the sports section of a broadsheet newspaper. Rewrite the forum post (Text C) for this audience.
4. Rewrite the newspaper article (Text D) as an email to a friend. You should write informally, using a chatty tone of voice, but remember to write clearly and accurately.

You now need to start making decisions about the way you write for the audience of your controlled assessment task.

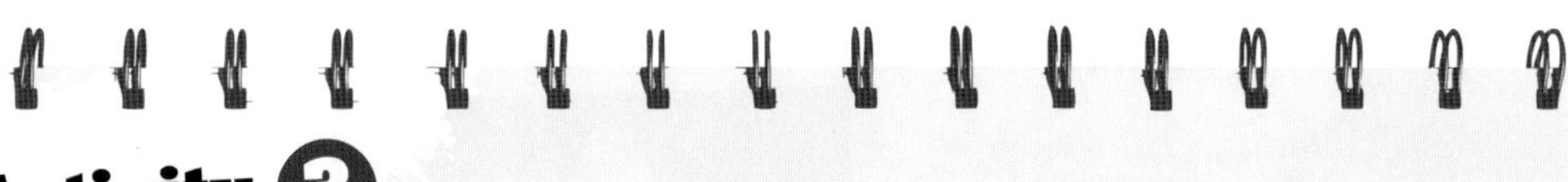

Activity 3

1. Find a text written for the audience that you have been asked to write for in your controlled assessment task.
   a) Highlight any words or phrases that are particularly suitable for the audience.
   b) Circle words and phrases that show the register of the piece of writing.
2. List the decisions that the writer has made to make the writing suitable for the intended audience.
3. Write a paragraph for a different text aimed at the audience you will have to write for.

ResultsPlus
Watch out!

When writing for people of your own age it is still important to write accurately. Avoid text language and the overuse of slang. A lively and jokey style is much better than too many incomplete sentences and words that your marker might not recognise!

3 Form

This lesson will help you to...

→ understand how form can reveal how and what to write

The controlled assessment writing task will tell you which form you should write in. The form is the type of text, such as a blog, an article or a podcast script. Different forms of writing have different rules, or **conventions**, that help us to recognise what type of text they are.

Look at these examples of forms that you could be asked to write.

Text A: Newspaper article

OKEHAMPTON TIMES

Established 1976

No: 1720

8 East Street, Okehampton, EX20 1AS. Tel: 01837 53641 THURSDAY, SEPTEMBER 3, 2009 www.okehampton-today.co.uk 55p

The race is on!

Towns set for terrific spectacle of Tour of Britain cycling event

by Alison Stephenson

SPEEDING cycles among a sea of Union flags – that's what Okehampton and Hatherleigh will look like when the penultimate leg of the Tour of Britain cycle race hits the streets in two weeks' time.

There will be huge

excitement as the adrenaline-charged spectacle comes to town on Friday, September 18 and the mayor is urging everyone to join in with cheering and flag waving as Okehampton takes centre stage in the prestigious race.

Okehampton Town Council has sent letters to the college and

primary school, inviting children to line the route where 100 cyclists will race through at speeds of up to 40mph in stage seven of the UK tour, which will be televised nationally and globally.

Town mayor David Weekes said: 'It's going to be exciting to see something like this.

'We are hoping for a

Andrei Burton jumping the famous tar barrels and a mini carnival procession with a special crepe paper float featuring a three-metre high racing bike by the boys and girls of Hatherleigh Carnival.

Bridge Street is likely to be closed until midday. A route around the north and east of the town will

especially after British riders did so well in this year's Tour de France. Some of those riders will be taking part in this event, and are expected to do well.

'We are anticipating a large crowd turning out to watch and cheer the riders on.'

The race will come

them the only safe way to get them through the town is to stop all the traffic and then clear the roads completely.

'If anyone has ever seen the Tour de France live or on TV they will see that this is what the French authorities do. It makes sense to follow a similar policy, given the French police's

will serve to raise the profile of the town.

'I know this will cause some people some inconvenience, but it is going to happen, and we intend to make sure it goes smoothly and with no risk to the public, motorists or the riders themselves.'

If anyone requires

INSIDE:

GCSE delight at college – page 3

Scene set for a grisly murder – page 3

Campaign to seek Fair Trade status – page 5

Not your average brown trout . . . – page 13

How battling Bridestowe

Text B: Letter

PeTA

PEOPLE FOR THE ETHICAL TREATMENT OF ANIMALS
501 FRONT ST.
NORFOLK, VA 23510
757-622-PETA
757-622-0457 (FAX)
PETA.org
info@peta.org

August 17, 2004

Dan Wyant, Director
Michigan Department of Agriculture
P.O. Box 30017
Lansing, MI 48909

Dear Mr. Wyant:

People for the Ethical Treatment of Animals (PETA) is the world's largest animal rights charity, with more than 800,000 members and supporters. We are writing to ask that your department regulate the methods by which animals used for fur are killed. Our request comes on the heels of an investigation we conducted into a chinchilla "farm" in Midland operated by Robin and Julie Ouderkirk. The Ouderkirks also sell chinchillas to laboratories and pet stores. On the enclosed video, Mr. Ouderkirk demonstrates how he kills these small animals... This method of electrocution (head to toe) is condemned by the American Veterinary Medical Association (AVMA) because it causes horrendous suffering.

The Michigan Department of Agriculture's "Generally Accepted Agricultural and Management Practices for the Care of Farm Animals," says that minks and foxes raised for fur should be killed "as quickly and painlessly as possible." No mention is made of chinchillas, and the publication is simply a guideline with no regulatory authority or enforcement behind it.

We believe that states that contain fur farms should ensure that animals are not being cruelly killed, as they are at the Ouderkirks' farm... We have also asked that the U.S. Department of Agriculture take on oversight of fur farms (see enclosed letter). Until it does, we hope that you will agree that there should be a limit to the cruelty that humans are allowed to impose on animals used for fur and that states should regulate animal care and killing on fur farms.

Thank you for your attention to this matter. I can be reached at 757-962-8334 if your office has questions. We look forward to your response.

Respectfully,

Mary Beth Sweetland

Mary Beth Sweetland, Senior Vice President
Director, Research & Investigations Department

AN INTERNATIONAL ORGANIZATION DEDICATED TO PROTECTING THE RIGHTS OF ALL ANIMALS

Text C: Blog

The Daily Woof

Dedicated to our four legged friends, stop on by our water dish to get daily digs on canine news, stories, and services from around the world.

Pets in the News:

Press of Atlantic City (blog) - Go greyhound

TDW Social Networking

Tweet this

Share this on Facebook

Get this for your site

Bark Outs

Posts

Comments

The Daily Woof

-CHIEF BARKER- RSM, CA, UNITED STATES *Head Muttin Charge.*

SEPTEMBER 21, 2009

7 Excellent iPhone Apps for Dog Lovers

-By Mary Ward

There is no end to what you can do with your passion and love for dogs, and these applications prove just that. You can find some excellent iPhone apps to keep your dog entertained and keep your skills sharp in caring for your pooch.

1. Dog Whistler - This gives you the perfect tool for dog training, all at your fingertips! You can use this app as a dog whistle to help train your dog and teach them tricks. This is a perfect complement to obedience training or helpful for the older dog set, making this one of the most popular iPhone apps out there.

Text D: Leaflet

WHAT'S WRONG WITH CRATING?

- **No, a crate will not help a puppy learn to "hold it."** Puppies' bladders are not fully developed until they are 4 to 6 months old, so trying to force them to learn something that they are incapable of learning can backfire.
- **No, crates do not promote a feeling of security.** On the contrary, many dogs who are "crate trained" for long periods develop separation anxiety, depression, hyperactivity, and other types of anti-social behavior.

Using an exercise pen, gating off a puppy-proofed room, tethering your puppy to you, making arrangements with a dog walker during the day, putting in a doggie door, going home at lunchtime and not working late, providing interactive toys (such as Kongs), and deciding that your couch isn't more important than your relationship with your dog are all better options than a crate. But mostly, puppies and dogs just need consistent, attentive, knowledgeable training and care—just as children do—not warehousing in a crate.

Activity 1

1 Look at each of the texts on page 58. Describe the features such as headings, headlines, use of text colour and paragraph length that help you to recognise what type of text it is.

The form of writing you are asked to produce can also affect how you write. A letter, for instance, is directed at one person so you would use direct address, whereas a newspaper article would use the third person. Blogs tend to use quite informal language, but a newspaper report should be formal.

Activity 2

Read the extracts below from two speeches that aim to persuade people to recycle.

Speech 1: Recycling: It's Worth the Bother

We see recycling everywhere. But does it really work?

The basic principle of recycling is common sense: We are told, 'if we all recycle, we'll reduce the strain on our Planet, and we'll save our money, our health and our environment.' But when you delve into the details, it's not always clear if we're making savings or not. In fact some people insist that it may all be futile. So what is the truth? Is recycling worth the bother?

Speech 2: You Can Change the World – Become an Activist

People, I want to ask you a question: do you think everything in your life is perfect just as it is? Or are there some changes you would make if you had the chance? If the answer is 'yes'... then you have everything you need to be an activist. Let me explain. A lot of people choose to sail steadily through life on an even keel. But there are some people who are boat rockers.

1 Compare the two texts. How are they similar in the way that they are written? For instance, how formal are they?

2 Using what you have learned about conventions:

a) write the opening to a speech about an issue that is important to you
b) write the opening to a letter to a relevant organisation on the same issue.

3 Describe the changes of form that you made when writing the opening to the letter compared with writing the opening to the speech.

When writing for a specified form it can be helpful to investigate what similar texts include and what choices the writers made. This will guide you in how to write your own text.

Activity 3

1 **Find examples of texts in the form that you have to write in for your controlled assessment task. It will be useful if you find examples that are on a similar theme to your task.**

2 **Copy and complete this table.**

What sort of vocabulary do the texts use?	*e.g. informal/formal*
What sort of sentences do the texts use?	*e.g. short/long, direct/indirect address, questions, exclamations*
How are the texts organised?	*e.g. headings, paragraphs, address lines, subject lines, bullet points*
What else do you notice about the form?	*e.g. coloured text*

You have now explored each instruction given to you in the task. You should be clear about what to include in your writing and how you should write.

Activity 4

1 **Review the choices you have made for purpose, audience and form. Write an email of one paragraph to your teacher summarising the decisions you should make when responding to the task you have been set.**

Here is an example of a controlled assessment task you could be expected to answer.

In your response to this task you would be expected to write using the conventions, or features, of an article.

Write an article for your school magazine in which you explain why school is important to you.

(20 marks)

Activity 5

Write the opening two paragraphs of the article explaining why school is important to you.

You should focus on using the right conventions, or features, of an article.

You should spend 20 minutes on this task.

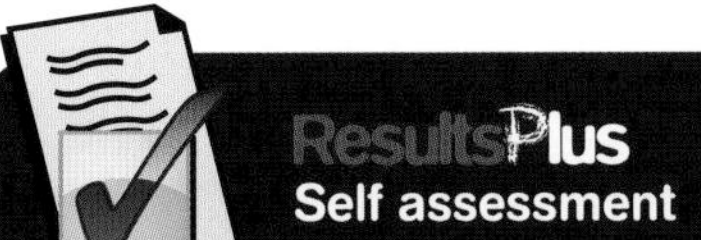

ResultsPlus Self assessment

Before you complete this self-assessment activity, you might like to read some sample answers to this task on the following pages (62-63).

1 **Check your answer to Activity 5:**
- Did you include a headline for your article?
- Did you give all the background details for your article in the opening paragraph?
- Did you select an appropriate tone for your article?
- Did you use a variety of sentences that are common in articles?

2 **Now try to grade your answer to Activity 5 by applying the mark scheme opposite. You will need to be careful and precise in your marking.**

Band 2
- ideas are appropriate to an article
- selects vocabulary well at times
- some control over sentence structure

Band 3
- ideas are appropriate to an article and effectively developed
- vocabulary is well-chosen
- evidence of crafting when constructing sentences

Band 4
- ideas are presented effectively as an article and sustained throughout
- vocabulary is aptly chosen
- well controlled, variety of sentences

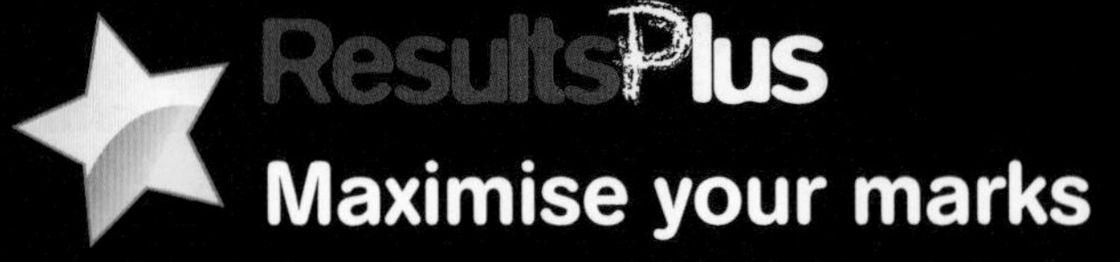

Maximise your marks

Write the opening two paragraphs of the article explaining why school is important to you. You should focus on using the right conventions, or features, of an article.

Here are three student answers to the article task on page 61. Read the answers together with the examiner comments around and after the answers. Then complete the activity.

Student 1 – Extract typical of a grade (D) answer

> This is an appropriate start to an article as it introduces the reader to the topic.

> The student is trying to keep the feel of an article but the repetition of 'I think' means this doesn't always feel like the appropriate tone.

School is important to me because I want to do well later in life and I want to make sure that I earn enough to look after me and my family and the people around me. I think it is important that I work hard for my exams and that I do other stuff that will look good on my CV.

I think school is important too because it means I get to meet up with my friends and we can have time to get to know each other and sometimes have fun.

> Sentences are fairly accurate but there is over use of 'I think' at the beginning of sentences.

Examiner summary

This part of the answer is typical of grade D performance. The student has done well to use a topic sentence at the beginning of each paragraph, which is typical of a newspaper article. The sentences and word choice show that the student is able to make some accurate choices but they tend to be repetitive. The use of 'I think' repeatedly makes the tone seem too personal for a newspaper article, even one intended for a school magazine.

Student 2 – Extract typical of a grade (C) answer

> 'We' is a good selection of word as it gives the article more authority.

> The first paragraph introduces the topic and this topic sentence shows the student is developing the idea.

School: What's the point?

We attend school every day from early in the morning through to late afternoon. We spend more time with our teachers than we do with our parents in term time! Is it really worth the hassle?

The obvious answer is yes, school is very important. We work hard at school and then we get good grades. There are lots of things that we need to learn that will help us become successful in later life. We will earn more money and we will be able to find lots of ways to make ourselves happy.

> Some evidence of control over sentences.

Examiner summary

This part of the answer is typical of grade C performance. The use of 'we' is a good word choice, as it makes the article sound like it has a lot more authority. The use of an exclamation and a question adds some evidence of control to the article and helps to introduce the issue in an interesting way. The second paragraph becomes a little more repetitive but the student has developed an idea appropriately from a topic sentence.

Student 3 – Extract typical of a grade B answer

An effective opening that grabs the reader immediately. This idea is carried on throughout the article. To engage the reader this way is important when writing a newspaper article.

Jail or Gateway?

Our school: a tall, red brick building that looms over the concrete yard. Frames criss-cross the towering windows and padlocks hang from doors and gates... It's possible that if they want us to stop viewing school as a prison that they should stop building them to look like some hideous torture chamber! In all seriousness – is this place just a jail for children or is it our gateway to the future we need.

Endless generations of kids have sat staring out of windows wishing for the bell to ring. The desire for freedom, to get out the uniform, to just... just... sit for hours in front of the television is too much for them. For these kids school has all the features of prison.

Some clever vocabulary makes the writer of the article sound like they are an authority.

Examiner summary

This part of the answer is typical of grade B performance. Opening with the description of the school as a jail is really effective. This is then sustained throughout. The choice of vocabulary makes the article sound like it has authority and the use of exclamations and ellipses show that the student has control over a variety of sentences.

ResultsPlus

Build better answers

Move from a Grade D to Grade C

In this part of your task you need think about the tone you need to create. Student 2 chose 'we' whilst student 1 chose 'I'. This small difference makes Student 2 sound more of an authority in the article, like it is something that you would read in a newspaper. Student 2 also develops the idea in the second paragraph rather than starting a new idea.

Move from a Grade C to Grade B

In this part of your task you need to use vocabulary and sentence choices to make your writing effective. Student 3 thought of an effective opening and then sustained this throughout. Although Student 2 used exclamations and questions in the first paragraph, Student 3 managed to use sentence variety in the whole of their response.

Putting it into Practice

1 **Write the opening two paragraphs of a blog about school.**

2 **Compare the choices you made for the article and the choices you made for the blog.**

4 Generating ideas

This lesson will help you to...

→ generate appropriate and engaging ideas to include in your writing

The first step in generating ideas is to identify the instructions in the task you have been given.

Activity 1

Look at this controlled assessment style writing task:

> Write an entry for a blog for your school website in which you describe a sporting event you have been involved in.

1 What is the subject of the piece of writing?

2 Who is the audience?

3 What is the purpose?

4 What form are you asked to write in?

You now have all the instructions you need to be able to start generating ideas. There is a range of strategies for getting initial ideas onto the page. You could:

- quickly brainstorm ideas and write down as many as you can on a sheet of paper
- create a spider diagram with the subject in the centre, arrows leading to different key ideas and notes on how to develop these
- list as many ideas as you can think of, with details the reader might like to know about each idea.

Brainstorm

Spider diagram

List

Activity 2

1 Use one of the strategies given above to generate ideas for the sporting event blog task from Activity 1.

2 Now choose a different strategy to generate ideas for an article for your school magazine describing a memorable holiday you have been on.

3 Evaluate which was the best strategy for you. Which one generated the most ideas? Which one gave you ideas that you think you could work with?

Before selecting the final ideas that you are going to use for the task, you need to extend each idea so that you have enough to write about. Think of more details than you need so you can select the best ones.

While researching, make a brief note of anything that you could include in your writing. Remember that you shouldn't directly use the writing of others in your work, as **plagiarism** is strictly forbidden.

Activity 3

Produce a mind map for the controlled assessment task you have been given.

1. **Generate three initial ideas that you might like to write about.**
2. **Add details to each of the ideas, then add thoughts and feelings.**
3. **Decide which idea gives you enough opportunity to produce a detailed and interesting piece of writing.**

Another strategy you could use is **research**. You should use books and the internet to find interesting stories, opinions, facts and ideas that you might include in your writing. You may need to look up some of your initial ideas as well, to see if there is further information you could include in your writing. This approach is particularly useful when your writing task is about factual events.

Activity 4

Using the ideas you generated in Activity 2 for the sporting event, carry out the following research tasks.

1. **List 5–10 key words or phrases you could type into an internet search engine to research: for instance, 'famous penalty shootouts'.**

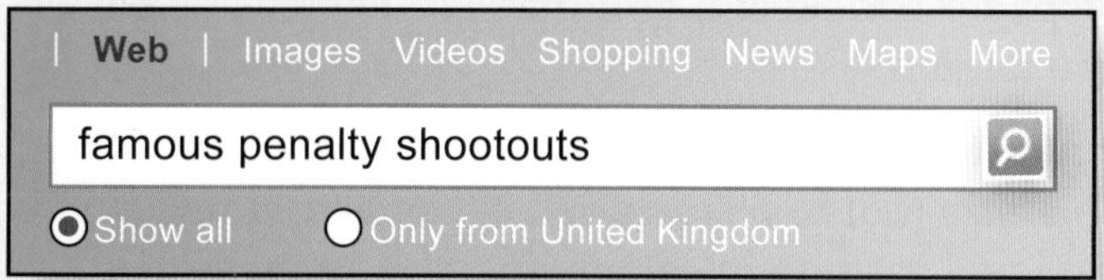

2. **List three questions that you would like to find the answers to, then research the answers: for example, 'How many international football tournament finals have been decided by penalty shootouts in the last twenty years?'**

5 Planning

This lesson will help you to...

→ select the best ideas to write about

→ organise these ideas into paragraphs

Before you begin to write your response to the controlled assessment task you need to decide exactly what you are going to write about. You should know what the ending will be before you write the first sentence.

Read the following plan for a film review of *Harry Potter and the Half-Blood Prince*, written for teenage film fans.

1 Background history of the film
- Box office smash
- More successful than Narnia

2 Brief reference to the story
- Harry vs Draco
- Slughorn
- Memories

3 Summary of the main focus of the film
- Relationships
- Child-like

4 Overall verdict on film
- Interesting to watch cast grow up
- Clumsy but ok
- Excellent special effects

In this plan each paragraph has a title and bullet points list what the paragraph will include. The plan is structured with an **introduction** (paragraph 1), **body** or development of points (paragraphs 2 and 3) and **conclusion** (paragraph 4). You should always use this as the basic structure for your writing.

Activity 1

1 Write a plan for a newspaper review of a film that you have watched recently. In the plan you should:

a) follow the basic structure of introduction, body and conclusion
b) give each paragraph a title (not to be included in the actual review)
c) bullet-point ideas you will include in each paragraph in the order you will write about them.

The way a text should be organised will depend on its purpose. For example, if you are writing to argue, the body of the writing should be organised around the different perspectives, for or against the idea.

Activity 2

Write a plan for an article arguing that the *Harry Potter* books are better than the films.

1 **Copy and complete this table giving two reasons 'for' and two reasons 'against' the argument that the books are better than the films.**

For	Against

2 **Under each reason you should bullet-point details you would include to support the idea.**

3 **Use your notes to create a plan for a piece of writing to argue for either the films or the books. Remember to plan the introduction and conclusion, as well as the body paragraphs.**

When writing to describe or explain, you might use chronological (time) order to organise the ideas or events. For example, when describing how your football team did last season, you would probably describe key moments starting at the beginning of the season and moving through to the end to say how they did overall.

Activity 3

Write a plan for a piece of writing to describe the events of your last summer holiday.

1 **Organise your ideas in chronological order, making notes under headings by week or at key points during the holiday.**

2 **Use the basic structure to create your plan, putting the events of your holiday into paragraphs.**

ResultsPlus
Controlled assessment tip

A lack of planning is the reason why many students lose marks. Without planning, you can forget to write clear paragraphs, run out of ideas or stray away from the topic. Having a plan means you know what each paragraph will say and where you will end up!

Activity 4

1 **Find texts that have a similar purpose to the controlled assessment task that you have been given. Give each paragraph of the texts you find a title and then bullet-point the ideas in each paragraph.**

2 **Summarise what you have learned about how you should plan your response to the controlled assessment writing task you have been given.**

3 **Create a plan for your task, using all that you have learned in this lesson.**

6 Openings

This lesson will help you to...

- → organise your ideas effectively
- → effectively open your writing

Your opening line should be interesting and engaging. It needs to hook the reader so that they want to read on. It should also be appropriate for the audience, purpose and form of the text for which you are writing.

Activity 1

Read the opening of this music review.

Album Reviews

nodzzz

There's a song on Nodzzz's 10-track, 16-minute long debut that sounds like young predators being let loose on the plains to rip flesh from bone with their bare teeth; in all its 59 seconds, 'Simple Song' whines with a two-note siren guitar while adenoidal singer Sean Paul (not that one) yelps like Brakes' Eamon Hamilton after diving into the primordial soup.

1 What features does it contain that make it suitable for its audience of young music fans?

2 Imagine that the audience for the review were adults, with little interest in modern music. Rewrite the opening in a way that would encourage this audience to read on.

3 Imagine that the purpose of the text was to persuade someone not to buy the album. Rewrite the opening.

Activity 2

Look at this controlled assessment style writing task.

Write an article for a music shop website in which you review your 10 favourite albums.

1 Copy and complete the table below. Evaluate each of the possible opening lines for effectiveness, giving them a score out of 10, and then explain your reasons.

2 Each of these openings use techniques that make them effective. Find examples of the following techniques:

a) question
b) direct address
c) ellipses
d) pattern of three.

3 Write your own opening line for the music shop website article.

Alternative opening lines	Score	Explanation
Only 10... really?		
Start the chart countdown music, cue cheesy DJ voice, introduce over-loud 'Num---ber 10!' and let's begin with the countdown...		
There is obviously the cool 10 albums, the ones that will have you music fans nodding wisely and assuring me – yes – those are the albums of choice and then there are the sinful, dare-I-admit-I-can't-live-without-you choices that will get me ridiculed: mm, how honest should I be?		

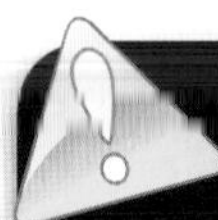

ResultsPlus Watch out!

Although the opening paragraph is important in gaining the attention of the reader, the closing paragraph is also very important. Be careful to not run out of energy and enthusiasm in the last paragraph. Write a final sentence that will have a powerful effect on the reader!

You should use similar techniques when writing the opening sentence of each body paragraph. These **topic sentences** indicate to the reader what the paragraph will be about. Look at the following paragraph from an email. The topic sentence uses direct address and immediately tells the reader what the paragraph will be about.

> You won't believe the wonderful summer I've had! First, I started sleeping in every day. Then, I would go swimming with my friends. I stayed up late watching TV a lot, and I also went to camp for a week. So, I wished my summer would never end!

The topic sentence 'You won't believe the wonderful summer I've had!' uses direct address to open the paragraph. The reader knows immediately that the rest of the paragraph (the supporting sentences) will explain why the writer has had such a good summer.

To help the reader move through the piece of writing, the paragraph also uses **discourse markers** in the supporting sentences – 'First', 'Then', 'also', 'So'. The discourse markers you should use depend on the purpose of your writing as shown in this table.

To add information		
and equally	moreover therefore	furthermore also
To make comparisons		
similarly also although in contrast both	likewise again however and on the other hand	on the contrary yet whereas but conversely
To sequence		
firstly while	secondly meanwhile	finally before
To add examples		
such as	for instance	for example
To summarise and conclude		
in summary	in conclusion	therefore

Activity 3

Look at this controlled assessment style writing task.

> **Write the script for a podcast for a teenagers' website, in which you review your favourite computer game.**

1. Write three different opening lines for the script, each using a different technique chosen from the list in Activity 2.
2. Evaluate how effective each opening is, then choose one to be the opening of the first paragraph.
3. Complete the paragraph of the script using sentences with appropriate discourse markers.
4. Write the opening line of each body paragraph, using topic sentences.

ResultsPlus Self assessment

Check your answer – have you:

- used at least one of the techniques that captures the readers' attention?
- used topic sentences that signpost to the reader what the paragraph will be about?

7 Crafting vocabulary

This lesson will help you to...

→ **make appropriate and effective vocabulary choices.**

Selecting the right vocabulary for your controlled assessment task is not about finding the longest words. You need to find the words that are the most appropriate to the task you have been given. Pitching your vocabulary at the right level for your audience is very important.

Activity 1

1 Look at this controlled assessment style writing task and identify the audience.

> **Write a blog for your school's website in which you comment on the importance of friendship.**

Now read this extract from a response to this task.

> *Friendship is a significant component of human existence that we would do well to truly comprehend and appreciate. Some people believe 'the righteous friend' is the one whom you trust and to whom you can confide all your secrets. Others define that person as one who stands by your side in sorrow and in joy alike. Although opinions vary on the definition of friendship, all tend to concur that friendship is integral to human psychological well-being.*

2 Identify the words and phrases in the response that are inappropriate for the audience.

3 Rewrite the extract in your own words, selecting vocabulary that is appropriate to the blog's audience.

Remind yourself of the language choices, including register, that need to be considered when writing for different audiences.

Activity 2

1 Write a paragraph for each of the following audiences, explaining that friendship is more important than anything else. Vary the vocabulary and register you use appropriately.

a) a friend
b) a parent
c) an anti-bullying charity website

ResultsPlus
Controlled assessment tip

Don't avoid difficult words in your writing because you think that you will spell them wrong. Give the word a go and get the credit for being interesting and including effective vocabulary choice.

When selecting vocabulary, you also need to choose words that help to achieve the purpose of the text. For example, if writing to inform, your vocabulary would probably be concise, whereas descriptive writing may use more expressive words.

Whatever your purpose for writing, being able to choose accurate and precise vocabulary is an important skill.

Activity 3

Here is part of a letter to a charity website arguing about the importance of friendship over self-defence against bullying.

Complete the following tasks to rewrite the paragraph so that vocabulary is used more precisely.

> You mention in your article that friendship wasn't as important as being able to stick up for yourself. Being able to stick up for yourself is quite good but friendships stop you from having to go against other people because they tend to leave you alone. I am very happy when I am with people as they make me feel really safe. Friendships stop bullying so are far more important than trying to be strong by yourself.

1 Change the highlighted verbs so that they are more concise: for example, you could change 'stick up for' to 'protect'.

2 Choose synonyms for any repeated words.

3 Choose more descriptive synonyms for the underlined adjectives so that they can be expressed in one word: for instance, change 'very happy' to 'content'.

Writers often 'craft' their writing – changing and testing out different vocabulary to see which combination is the most effective.

Activity 4

1 Write a paragraph for the controlled assessment task in Activity 1.

Spend 10 minutes trying out different words until:

a) you have chosen the correct vocabulary for audience and purpose

b) you have used precise vocabulary.

8 Crafting sentences

This lesson will help you to...

- → understand the range of sentence types and structures
- → use different sentences types to create specific effects

Sentences can take many forms, from a simple command, like 'Run!', to a complex sentence using several clauses. There are also different types of sentence, such as questions and exclamations. Knowing how to use a variety of sentences to achieve the right effect, will make your writing more effective. You need to be able to use the following sentence structures and types confidently.

Sentence structures:

- A **simple** sentence consists of nouns and a verb: 'The cat sat on the mat.'
- A **compound** sentence is two independent clauses joined together by **coordinators**, words like *and/as/for/so*: 'He was working, so I went out.'
- A **complex** sentence is a simple sentence with a dependent clause, usually separated from the main sentence by a comma: 'I wanted to challenge him, since I knew he was lying.'

Types of sentence:

- **Question**: 'Where are you going?'
- **Exclamation**: 'You might be next!'
- **Command**: 'Boil the kettle.'
- **Statement**: 'There are ten new entries in the download chart.'

Activity 1

Find examples of the sentence types and structures listed above in the following extract.

Charlotte wanted to go shopping. It was Saturday and the weather was pretty bad, so it seemed like a good way to pass the afternoon, but her mother was too busy to give her a lift. 'Go and ask your father,' she suggested. 'Where is he?' Charlotte asked. 'I don't know!' said her mother. 'Try the garden.' Charlotte went outside, checked the garden, and found her father in the shed. 'Mum says you must give me a lift to the shops,' she said.

Using a variety of simple, complex and compound sentences allows you to change the pace of your writing. For example, in descriptive writing:

- long, complex sentences speed up the pace to describe action scenes
- short, simple sentences slow down the pace to create suspense.

Simple sentences, statements and commands are useful when you need to convey small chunks of information at a time. They are often used in informative or persuasive writing, for example:

'Sleep is vital for your body to function.'

Asking a question will make the reader think about the answer. You can then go on to answer it – perhaps in an unexpected way. For example:

'Why should you buy this game? ... Honestly, you shouldn't; it's not worth it.'

Rhetorical questions work particularly well in persuasive writing, for example:

'If this is true, can you afford not to get enough sleep?'

Varying the sentence structure and type also keeps your reader interested and stops the writing from feeling repetitive.

Activity 2

Read the paragraph below about the environment. It contains only simple sentences used as statements. It is informative but not very interesting to read.

1 **Add to and edit the sentences to make the extract more interesting to read and to explain the reasons for the difficulty in recycling. For instance, you could use complex sentences or use questions to raise issues.**

2 **Add to and edit the sentences to make the extract persuasive. For instance, try adding commands and exclamations.**

> The confusion over what we can and cannot recycle continues to confuse consumers. Plastics are especially troublesome. Different types of plastic require different processing to be reformulated and re-used as raw material. Some towns accept all types of plastic for recycling. Other towns only accept jugs, containers and bottles stamped with certain numbers.

Activity 3

Write a paragraph in response to this controlled assessment style writing task:

Write the script for a podcast for a website for young people aged 11-14, where you inform them about an environmental issue.

1 **Experiment with the different types and structures of sentence that you can use. Try writing two different versions of the same paragraph.**

2 **Edit your paragraph, making sure it is varied and fit for the purpose and audience.**

Check your answer – have you:

- written sentences that are accurate?
- chosen a variety of sentences?
- used sentences that have an effect on the reader?

9 Crafting punctuation

This lesson will help you to...

- → select a range of punctuation
- → select punctuation for effect

Punctuation makes the meaning of a text clear for the reader, by acting as a signpost to tell the reader how to read it. You will be expected to show that you can use a range of punctuation accurately in your writing.

Full stop	I am a boy.
Comma	I walked to the station, passing by the store on the way.
Apostrophe	The cat's toy / I didn't do it
Exclamation mark	Get up!
Question mark	What should I do?
Speech marks	"I am going to go away now," said the poor man.
Semicolon	John was hurt; Jack was upset.
Colon	There are many reasons, including:
Brackets	I walked silently so she wouldn't hear me (I hoped).
Ellipses	Then it all went quiet...
Dash	You're right – at least I think you are.

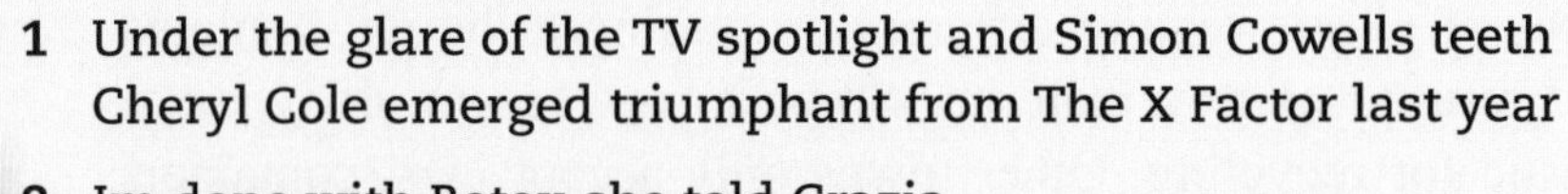

Activity 1

Punctuate the following sentences.

1 **Under the glare of the TV spotlight and Simon Cowells teeth Cheryl Cole emerged triumphant from The X Factor last year**

2 **Im done with Botox she told Grazia**

3 **Dannii has upped the ante with a new do a face flattering glossy grown up chin length bob that she has played around with quiff side parting wavy poker straight and hairband**

Punctuation can also create effects that help you to achieve the text's purpose. For instance, in persuasive writing, writers often use a lot of question marks and exclamation marks to suggest the reader should feel some emotion. Exclamation marks would also be used in a text to entertain. Writing to comment, inform or analyse might include more commas, linking additional information to sentences to add depth.

Activity 2

1 The same words can be used in different texts, even if they have different purposes. Punctuate the following text in two different ways for two different purposes:

a) to inform
b) to entertain.

It is a five day show with over €900000 in prize money on offer It has attracted a world class field for the showing competitions Ireland's finest show jumpers and the top ten show jumping teams in the world Belgium France Germany Great Britain Ireland Italy Switzerland the Netherlands and the United States of America €599000 of the overall prize money is dedicated to the 12 international jumping competitions

spread over the five days of the show visitors are assured of seeing some of the finest show jumping in the world

Activity 3

Write a paragraph for this controlled assessment writing task.

Write an article for a computer game magazine in which you describe your ideas for a new computer game.

1 Write two different versions, one for the purpose given to you in the task and one for another purpose of your choice. Use at least three different types of punctuation in each version that are appropriate to the purpose.

2 Explain how your choices affect how the reader might respond to the text.

Assessment Practice

Here is an example of a controlled assessment task you could be expected to answer. In your response to this task you will be expected to use punctuation effectively.

Write the first entry of a blog to inform teenagers about a trip that you have taken. (20 marks)

Activity 4

Write the opening paragraph of the blog for teenagers. Focus on the variety and effectiveness of the punctuation that you use.

You should spend 20 minutes on this task.

ResultsPlus Self assessment

Before you complete this self-assessment activity, you might like to read some sample answers to this task on the following pages (76-77).

1 **Check your answer to Activity 4:**
- Did you use full stops and capital letters accurately?
- Did you use other punctuation such as question marks, speech marks, exclamation marks, apostrophes and commas?
- Have you used punctuation to control the meaning and the effect on the reader?

2 **Now try to grade your answer to Activity 4 by applying the mark scheme opposite. You will need to be careful and precise in your marking.**

■ **Band 2**
- uses punctuation that has some impact on the reader and makes some important ideas stand out
- sentences are mostly accurate, with some control over the way the reader reads the text

● **Band 3**
- uses punctuation that has an impact on the reader and makes important ideas stand out
- includes clear and accurate sentences, with control over the way the reader reads the text

▲ **Band 4**
- uses punctuation precisely to create the effects intended
- includes well structured sentences, with effective control over the way the reader reads the text

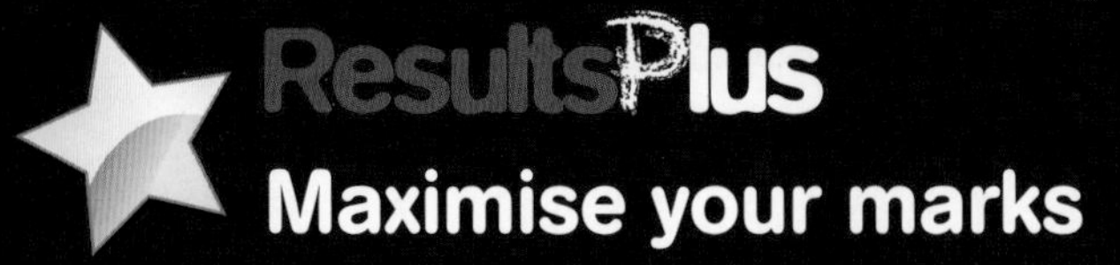

ResultsPlus
Maximise your marks

Write the first entry of your blog to inform teenagers of a trip you are taking.

Write the opening paragraph of the blog to teenagers. You should focus on the effective use of punctuation.

Here are three student answers to the blog task on page 75. Read the answers together with the examiner comments around and after the answers. Then complete the activity.

Student 1 – Extract typical of a grade (D) answer

Mostly clear and accurate sentences.

My reason for going on the trip was that I needed a break I wanted to get away from all the stress of work and I wanted to experience the Spanish way of life. I hope to see a few historic moments in the capital city of Madrid and also go to the Camp Nou which is the home of Barcelona to watch a football game. Also I would like to visit some of the costas to discover the night life and also to see the beautiful fishing villages and Mr Tiagi an information desk worker in Spain said "I moved over because the country and all the places in it are so amazing and I wanted to live my life here."

Some punctuation to show speech.

Examiner summary

This part of the answer is typical of grade D performance. The student has punctuated the sentences accurately for the most part and there is some attempt to show expression in the writing with the use of speech marks. The opening sentence shows some attempt to sound excited by the trip and expression would have been helped with an exclamation mark.

Student 2 – Extract typical of a grade (C) answer

Good use of the comma to give the effect of speech.

A dash is used to give the effect of a pause – connecting the list to his views on the hotel.

Hi everybody, I am just writing to tell you what I have done so far in Italy. Yesterday I arrived at the airport. It was a bit hot; it felt as if I was melting. I then went to find my hotel, wasting a bit of money in taxis. I found my hotel, it was ok – nice view, great food and one of the coolest swimming pools in the world. Are you worried about me yet? I know I am a long way from home but this blog should keep you informed of the trips I make. As you can see Spain was a hoot and I reckon Italy is gonna be amazing... once I figure out how to order some of the ice cream.

This should really be a semi-colon – so there is a need for a greater variety of punctuation.

Examiner summary

This part of the answer is typical of grade C performance. The comma after 'Hi everybody,' helps the writing sound as if it is spoken language, which is effective in a blog. The use of the dash and the list separated by commas also shows that the student is thinking about how this would be spoken – and gives the intended effect of capturing what the hotel is like. The student missed opportunities to use the semi-colon, which means the use of punctuation is not as precise as it should be.

Student 3 – Extract typical of a grade B answer

Some variety of punctuation, which supports the intended effect of greeting the audience enthusiastically.

Hello guys! I just thought I'd inform you of a trip that I have planned abroad. I have many reasons for going on my trip with one example would be the landscape. Scientist George McCann said, "When we experimented on the soil in Italy we found it was the most delicate soft soil we have ever seen. This is due to the wonderful care that the farmers put into the farms. This makes the landscape of Italy truly wonderful!" In my trip I hope to understand this perfect landscape and its historical traditions.

Sentences are accurately structured.

Examiner summary

This part of the answer is typical of grade B performance. The use of punctuation is precise, with the inclusion of commas and apostrophes, and the sentences are well structured. The use of the exclamation marks is intended to give the effect of excitement. To improve the answer further the student could use punctuation to make the writing seem a little less formal – for example, including dashes and ellipses to show how we pause and connect ideas when speaking. This would give the impression that they were writing a blog.

ResultsPlus

Build better answers

Move from a Grade D to Grade C

In this part of your task you need to employ punctuation accurately. Student 1 writes with a lot of enthusiasm about Spain, but some of the sentences are not punctuated accurately. Although inaccurate in places, Student 2 manages to use more of a variety of punctuation to help give the piece of writing expression.

Move from a Grade C to Grade B

In this part of your task you need to use punctuation for effect. Student 3 has employed punctuation precisely throughout the response, and has also included exclamation marks and speech marks to ensure the intended effect of the blog. Student 2 has more sense of being spoken language and if they had used semi-colons accurately they may have achieved more than Student 3, who seems a little formal at times for a blog.

Putting it into Practice

1 **Revisit the opening paragraph for your blog. Experiment by including lots of different punctuation marks. Assess each time if the punctuation you have included is a) accurate and b) effective.**

Controlled Assessment Practice

Examiner's tip

Your controlled assessment will be based on a theme. Your writing task will be on the same theme as the texts you have studied for the reading part of this unit.

Guidance for students: Writing Task

What do I have to do?
You will complete one writing task on the theme of the environment.
You must complete this task on your own.

How much time do I have?
Following preparation, you will have up to two hours to complete the task.

Examiner's tip

Deciding on the answers to these elements will help you plan your writing.

How do I prepare for the task?

- Select one task.
- You will be provided with guidance about writing, which may include:
  - the content – real or imagined
  - the audience and purpose
  - the form and structural features of writing
  - the 'voice' you may want to use
  - appropriate language techniques.
- You should then prepare by making notes and planning your response to the task.

Examiner's tip

Remember to check over your writing before submitting it.

What must the response to the task show?
Your response must show that you can:

- make choices in writing that are appropriate to audience and purpose
- spell, punctuate and use grammatical structures that are accurate and appropriate for purpose and effect.

How should I present the response?
A written response of up to 1000 words.

The Writing Task for the student

Complete one task from those below.

EITHER

Write an article for a magazine in which you persuade readers about an environmental issue from a specific point of view. (20)

OR

Write the script for a podcast for a website for young people aged 11-14, where you inform them about an environmental issue. (20)

Examiner's tip

Pick one task here. Remember to make your response appropriate for the given audience, purpose and form.

Unit 2 The Writer's Craft The Writer's Voice

Whether you are taking GCSE English or GCSE English Language, this unit will help you to prepare for the writing task in your examination (Section B in English Language and Section C in English). This task will ask you to write a response to a situation, issue or problem and you'll need to be able to use evidence to support the views and opinions you write about.

This section of the book will help you to build on the writing skills you developed in Unit 1, giving you plenty of strategies for writing effectively under time constraints in an exam. The following lessons explore different ways that you can approach the writing task. The activities you'll complete in this unit are all focused on helping you to achieve the best grade you can in this section of the examination.

Your assessment

Unit 2 is an examination unit. The first part of your examination will focus on the set texts you have studied in class, and the final section will be a writing task which is the focus of this unit of the book. You will have to answer one question from a choice of **two**.

Your response to the writing section must show that you can:

- ✔ reflect on ideas, issues, experiences and events, rather than writing a narrative or description
- ✔ write in a form, such as a newspaper article, formal report or magazine review, targeting a specified audience
- ✔ reflect and comment on contemporary issues, situations or problems that are relevant to you, such as lifestyle, school or college life, local issues or national issues that affect young people.

Assessment Objectives

Your response to this section of the examination will be marked using these Assessment Objectives:

- ✔ **Write clearly, effectively and imaginatively, using and adapting forms and selecting vocabulary appropriate to the task and purpose in ways that engage the reader.**
- ✔ **Organise information and ideas into structured and sequenced sentences, paragraphs and whole texts, using a variety of linguistic and structural features to support cohesion and overall coherence.**
- ✔ **Use a range of sentence structures for clarity, purpose and effect, with accurate punctuation and spelling.**

This student book unit will help you to understand what these require you to do so that you can write a successful response in the examination.

1 Purpose

This lesson will help you to...

→ understand how to write for different purposes

When you look at the writing task in the examination, you need to work out what **purpose** you are being asked to write for. You need to make the right choices as you write to achieve this purpose.

Look at the table below, which lists many of the purposes that you might be asked to write for.

Purpose	Definition
Argue	To present views on an issue
Persuade	To make readers think or do something
Inform	To give information about something
Describe	To create a picture in the reader's mind
Explain	To offer reasons about how and why something happens or works
Comment	To give your opinion on a topic
Review	To tell the reader about something (e.g. a film) and give your opinion
Advise	To offer suggestions or recommendations
Analyse	To examine in detail in order to discover meaning

Activity 1

Read the extracts opposite from three students' responses to tasks on the same theme but for different purposes.
The devices that have been used to achieve the purpose have been highlighted for you.

1 **Write a second paragraph to follow on from each extract about the things teenagers do for the local community. Continue to use the devices that have been highlighted.**

2 **Write a response to this task where the purpose is to describe:**

> **Write a newspaper article describing the things that teenagers do.**

Think carefully about the language choices you should make.

3 **Using the four extracts that you have read and written, copy and complete this table about the techniques used for different purposes. Some examples have been given.**

Purpose	What is written?	How is it written?
Persuade		Exclamation
Inform	Facts and statistics	
Argue		
Describe		

Task 1: Write a newspaper article **persuading** readers that the positive things teenagers do deserve reporting.

Why are we treated so badly? Shown by newspapers to be thugs, chavs, anti-social and ignorant: is this really fair?

Each day I slog hard and want to impress but nothing seems to make the same impact as some hoodie with a bottle of cider and a weapon!

rhetorical question
emotive language
rhetorical question
emotive language
exclamation
slang

Task 2: Write a newspaper article **to inform** readers about the positive things that teenagers do deserve reporting.

In this area 5 teenagers a year are reprimanded by the police.

52 teenagers have received some form of award for their talent or for their service to the community. Jake Tabb (14) won first prize in a national judo competition. Elsa Lacey (15) has had her collection of short stories published.

statistics
statement
evidence
statement

Task 3: Write a newspaper article **arguing** that the positive things teenagers do deserve reporting.

I understand that some teenagers let us down. They sit in gangs on corners, sipping from bottles of alcohol and scaring passers-by. You are right to consider the crimes of young people news.

However, do you think the balance of your reporting on teenagers is correct? I know of more young people who get it right than get it wrong but hear nothing about it in your newspaper.

direct address
connective
question

Identifying the purpose and using it to decide what you should write and how you should write should become part of your routine at the start of the examination.

ResultsPlus
Exam tip

Before writing on your answer booklet you should label the question on the examination paper. Highlight the purpose, audience and form and then scribble down notes to help you make the right choices.

Activity 2

Look at the following tasks.

A: Write an article for the school newspaper giving information about how students feel in the time leading up to examinations.

B: Write an article persuading teachers to be more sympathetic to how students feel in the time leading up to examinations.

1 Note down what and how you would write for each purpose.

2 Audience

This lesson will help you to...

→ understand how to write for different audiences

Different audiences want to read different things. They will also respond to different styles and registers of writing. Look at this task:

> **Write a letter to your local newspaper arguing that the positive things teenagers do should be reported.**

The audience for your writing is readers of the local newspaper. This means you are writing for adults you do not know.

Activity 1

Read the opening of the letter below and consider what the audience would want to know.

Hello

My name is Julie Shuttleton and I am 14 years old. I attend Fairfield High School and I am in Year 9 at the moment. I enjoy writing and making a difference. I am an active member of the school council and I do a lot of work to make sure that the people in my year group are treated fairly. I am writing this letter to argue that newspapers (like yours!) don't report the positive things that teenagers do. We shouldn't be made to look like thugs all of the time.

1. **How much of the information in the letter opening would adults who do not know the writer be interested in? Rewrite the opening, including only the details that the reader would want to know.**
2. **List any other details that are missing which you think would interest the reader.**

ResultsPlus
Exam tip

Remember that the audience of a piece of writing can be suggested in the form that has been selected for you. For instance, a school newspaper is likely to be aimed mostly at people who are students at the same school as you. A blog is likely to be aimed at people who know you well or it might simply be something you write for yourself.

It is important to consider not only *what* you write, but *how* you write for your audience. It is vital to adapt your style of writing and its **register** (how formal it is) to the audience. An email to a friend could be written informally; using slang and contractions, like 'what's': However a formal letter should use Standard English and more formal vocabulary.

Activity 2

The writer of the opening paragraph of the letter to the local newspaper in Activity 1 has made some errors in the register of her writing. At times she writes too informally for the audience.

1 **Identify the words or phrases that are too informal for an adult audience that the writer does not know.**

2 **For each one, suggest an alternative word or phrase that would create a more formal register.**

If you select the wrong register you could offend your audience or stop them from reading on because they don't think the text is meant for them.

ResultsPlus
Exam tip

In your examination, you also need to make sure that you are writing in a way that would impress an examiner. If you think the task requires the use of some informal language for effect then you may use it occasionally, but only where it clearly creates an effect. Slang, abbreviations and incomplete sentences should be avoided.

Activity 3

1 **For each of the following audiences, decide how formal or informal your writing would need to be. List the devices that you would use to help you achieve the correct register.**

a) friends **b) teacher** **c) politician**

2 **Write two paragraphs about the image of teenagers. Write one paragraph for people of your own age. Write one paragraph for your teacher.**

Identifying the audience and noting down what you should write and how you should write should become part of your routine at the start of the examination.

Activity 4

Look at the following tasks.

A: Write the text for a leaflet in which you inform 14- to 16-year-olds of places they could visit near you.

B: Write a blog for your school website in which you comment on the events that have taken place in your school over the past year.

1 For each task:

a) identify the audience

b) note down what and how you would write for this audience.

3 Understanding form

This lesson will help you to...

→ understand how to write in different forms

You could be asked to write in a range of different **forms**, including: a newspaper article, blog, letter, leaflet, speech or report.

There are rules or **conventions** that the reader expects to see when reading a particular type of text. For example, when reading a newspaper article the reader expects a headline and interviews with experts or witnesses.

Activity 1

1 Describe what you expect from each form in the following list. You could use some of the words and phrases in the box below to describe the conventions.

a) Newspaper article b) Leaflet c) Letter d) Blog e) Speech f) Magazine article

headlines	directed at the reader	informal language	formal language	facts
opinions	subheadings	light-hearted	interviews	organised as a story

2 Look at the three texts below. Identify the form of each and list the conventions.

Text A

OKEHAMPTON TIMES

Established 1976 No: 1720

8 East Street, Okehampton, EX20 1AS. Tel: 01837 53641 THURSDAY, SEPTEMBER 3, 2009 www.okehampton-today.co.uk 55p

The race is on!

Towns set for terrific spectacle of Tour of Britain cycling event

INSIDE:
GCSE delight at college – page 3
Scene set for a grisly murder – page 3
Campaign to seek Fair Trade status – page 5

by Alison Stephenson

SPEEDING cycles among a sea of Union flags – that's what Okehampton and Hatherleigh will look like when the penultimate leg of the Tour of Britain cycle race hits the streets in two weeks' time.

There will be huge excitement as the adrenaline-charged spectacle comes to town on Friday, September 18 and the mayor is urging everyone to join in with cheering and flag waving as Okehampton takes centre stage in the prestigious race.

Okehampton Town Council has sent letters to the college and primary school, inviting children to line the route where 100 cyclists will race through at speeds of up to 40mph in stage seven of the UK tour, which will be televised nationally and globally.

Town mayor David Weekes said: 'It's going to be exciting to see something like this.

'We are hoping for a really big turnout to encourage the cyclists.

'It's great for the town have a national event here and Devon as a whole and it will be good for the cycling industry here.'

The race will start in Hatherleigh which is a ...

For all your motoring needs
Vospers
All makes servicing, repairs and MOTs
01822-616407
West Devon Business Park, Tavistock

Text B

The Beautiful Game: Finding a Beckham of Bangladesh

Two budding journalists and documentary film makers, Ed and Waj, are about to take a trip to Bangladesh. Their mission? To record the exploits of the Bangladesh youth Football Academy, the lives of its thrity-five young apprentices, and its importance to the future of Bangladeshi football

SATURDAY, 16 JUNE 2007

Ed's Diary - Day 22 - 16.06.07:

Today was my last day in Bangladesh!!!

After an extensive lie-in this morning Howard came knocking on my hotel-room door and we went out shopping to buy presents for people, heading straight for Dhaka's top shopping mall (inside it was very much like a mall back in the States). I found yet another shop selling pirate DVDs so Howard and I both stocked up our movie collections, and then we bought some gifts for the Academy, for the people who'd been looking after us for the past few days, and for our friends back home.

At one o'clock we headed back to the hotel, checked out, loaded our

Blog Archive
▼ 2007 (26)
▼ June (18)
ONE FINAL NOTE TO YOU ALL
Ed's Diary - Day 15 - 09.06.07:
Ed's Diary - Day 14 - 08.06.07:
Ed's Diary - Day 13 - 07.06.07:
Ed's Diary - Day 12 - 06.06.07:
Ed's Diary - Day 11 - 05.06.07:
Ed's Diary - Day 10 - 04.06.07
Ed's Diary - Day 9 - 03.06.07
QUICK NOTE
► May (8)

Ed Danson - Journalist + Filmmaker

Text C

Kimberly Gower
24 Batchwood Drive
Durham City
Durham
DH1 4VP

The Manager
Bede Coffee Shop
14 Hawthorn Avenue
Durham City
Durham
DH1 4JA

3rd March 2010

Dear Sir/Madam,

RE: Advertisement for weekend work

I wish to apply for the Saturday waiting job as advertised in the window of the coffee shop. I have always loved spending time in Bede coffee shop, and would be a very enthusiastic employee!

I am 16 years old and studying for my GCSEs at the local high school. I am very keen to gain experience in the retail and hospitality industries as I hope to be accepted onto a catering course at a nearby college next year. I have received good marks in my mock GCSEs, including a B grade in Maths, and so would be confident with dealing with money.

In addition, I have been helping my Dad at car boot sales since a young age and am therefore very well-practised in being friendly to customers and getting up early at the weekend!

Attached is my CV with the contact details of people who are happy to give a character reference.

I look forward to hearing from you.

Yours faithfully,

Kimberly Gower

Understanding the conventions of a form is helpful in deciding what to include in a text. However, the conventions of different forms can change according to the purpose of the text. For instance, the language in a leaflet written to inform would be very different from the language in a leaflet aiming to persuade.

Activity 2

A blog is like a diary that recounts everyday events and opinions. Blogs are generally written as if the writer knows the audience. Look at the extract below from a journalist's blog in *The Guardian* that is commenting on Steven Seagal's new reality TV programme.

Written as if we are part of the same group as the writer. Therefore, it is personal.

Doesn't really use slang or abbreviations but uses punctuation and sentences to mimic the way she speaks.

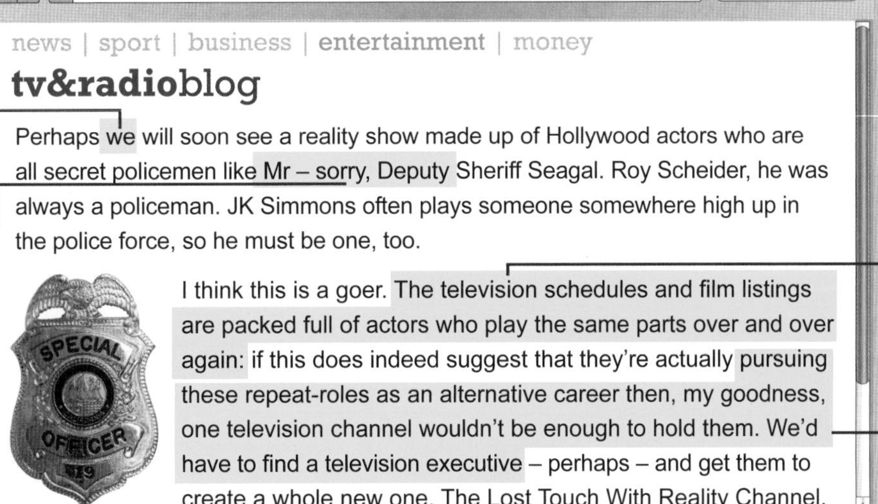

news | sport | business | entertainment | money

tv&radioblog

Perhaps we will soon see a reality show made up of Hollywood actors who are all secret policemen like Mr – sorry, Deputy Sheriff Seagal. Roy Scheider, he was always a policeman. JK Simmons often plays someone somewhere high up in the police force, so he must be one, too.

I think this is a goer. The television schedules and film listings are packed full of actors who play the same parts over and over again: if this does indeed suggest that they're actually pursuing these repeat-roles as an alternative career then, my goodness, one television channel wouldn't be enough to hold them. We'd have to find a television executive – perhaps – and get them to create a whole new one. The Lost Touch With Reality Channel.

Seems to be commenting on a bigger issue which makes this feel like a review or newspaper article, which is suitable for a news website.

High level vocabulary although with some humour, which gives it a more informal feel.

1 Write a paragraph from two different blogs:

a) recounting your evening's TV viewing for a blog on your school website
b) reviewing a TV programme for a blog on TV channel's website.

Try to use what you have learned from the journalist's blog and balance the informal conventions of a blog with the style of writing needed to achieve the purpose.

The conventions of forms like letters and emails, which are usually written for a specific audience, will change depending on who the intended reader is. A letter to a future employer and a letter to your parents would be very different.

Activity 3

1 Write two letters describing your life as a teenager – one letter to your teacher, the second to your friend.

How are the conventions of letters similar and different for the two audiences?

ResultsPlus
Watch out!

Be careful that you only write the text for the form you have been given. Although newspaper articles are often written in columns and include pictures, your examiner is only interested in the writing!

4 Form in action

This lesson will help you to...

→ **understand how form can tell you what and how to write in the exam**

Understanding why you should write different forms of text in a particular way with different forms will help you to remember to make good choices in the examination. The form has been removed from this task:

> Write ____________________ to request that the positive things teenagers do are reported too.

Below are the opening paragraphs of two responses to the task. One is an article for the local newspaper; the other is a letter to the editor of the local newspaper. The highlighted words and phrases show you what has been written and how.

SOCIAL TEENAGERS SCARE THE ELDERLY

Janice Hasell (89), resident of the Parkside Estate in Newport, complained to police because a gang of teenagers had congregated on her street corner. It was reported that she told police that the group were laughing in a threatening way.

It is hard to understand why someone would be afraid of a group of young people enjoying each others' company. It is likely something that Mrs Hasell used to spend her time doing when she was 15. Mrs Hasell could be blamed for being over-sensitive but her fear was so real that she needed to call for help. So, who should be seen as responsible for turning children into villains?

WHAT: Facts about the people involved in the story.

HOW: Third person, story about other people. The writer is not involved in the events.

WHAT: The writer's opinion.

HOW: Commenting on the events but trying to keep an impression of fairness and balance.

HOW: Questions raises further issues that the article is going to talk about.

Dear Sir

It has come to my attention that you present teenagers in an unfair way. Many of your reports show teenagers to be anti-social and violent. Do you think it is time to report the other side of the story?

There are many things that my friends and I do right but we never seem to make it into the pages of your newspaper.

WHAT: An opening greeting.

WHAT and HOW: Personal opinions that are stated quite strongly.

HOW: Direct address, the writer is talking directly to the reader.

HOW: Asking a question that the writer hopes the reader will respond to.

Activity 1

Look at the newspaper article and letter above.

1 Copy and complete the table below to explore the choices the writers have made.

	Decisions made	Why have these decisions been made?
Newspaper article	• *Third person address* •	• *Articles report what happened* •
Letter	• *Direct address* •	• *Gives impact to the argument* •

2 Write the next paragraph of the newspaper article and letter. Continue to use the same choices that have been made by the writers in these two forms.

The form you are writing in will affect how you organise your writing. For instance, a speech is written in continuous sentences and paragraphs with a greeting at the beginning and a sign off at the end, whereas the text for a leaflet is written with headings and subheadings.

ResultsPlus
Self assessment

Check your answer – have you:

- planned to use techniques that are appropriate for the text you are writing?
- considered a tone of voice that is suitable for the form you are writing?
- thought about how to structure the text in a way that is suited to the text you are writing?

Activity 2

1 Write extracts for each of the forms listed below, arguing that a positive image of teenagers should be publicised. You should write for a general adult audience. Think carefully about the way you organise your ideas and the register you select.

a) a blog b) the text for a website c) the text for a leaflet

2 Describe and explain the choices you have made.

Identifying the form and noting down what you should write and how you should write should become part of your routine at the start of the examination.

Activity 3

Look at these two tasks:

A: Write a speech to a group of foreign students describing your school life.

B: Write a blog for a teenage website for fans of The X-Factor, giving your thoughts on the judges' attitudes to the contestants.

For each task: Identify the form, then note down what and how you would write for the form. Make sure that your choices also match the audience and purpose in the brief.

5 Generating ideas

This lesson will help you to...

→ generate and develop appropriate and engaging ideas for your writing

In the examination, you will have only a limited amount of time to complete your writing task. You will have to come up with ideas **quickly** for a task you have never seen before. To make sure you can generate interesting and imaginative ideas under pressure, you need to develop a strategy that will help you get started. You should begin by looking closely at the task that you have been given.

Activity 1

Look at the following task:

> **Write the text for a speech to the school council in which you review the school's approach to homework.**

Quickly answer these questions:

1 What is the subject of the piece of writing?
2 What is the purpose?
3 Who is the audience?
4 What form are you writing in?

Having identified the purpose, audience and form, you should focus on the subject of the task you have been given.

There are several strategies you can use to get started when considering what to write, including spider diagrams, lists and mind maps.

Lists

HOMEWORK
- IDEA 1
  - — other detail
  - — emotions
  - — perspectives
- IDEA 2
  - —
  - —
  - —
- IDEA 3
  - —
  - —
  - —

Spider diagrams

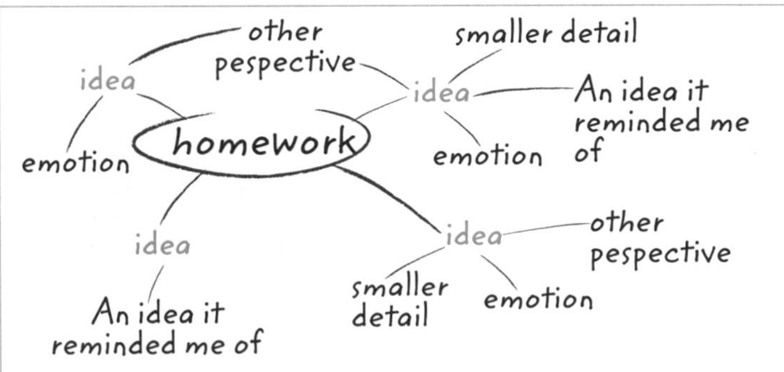

Mind mapping

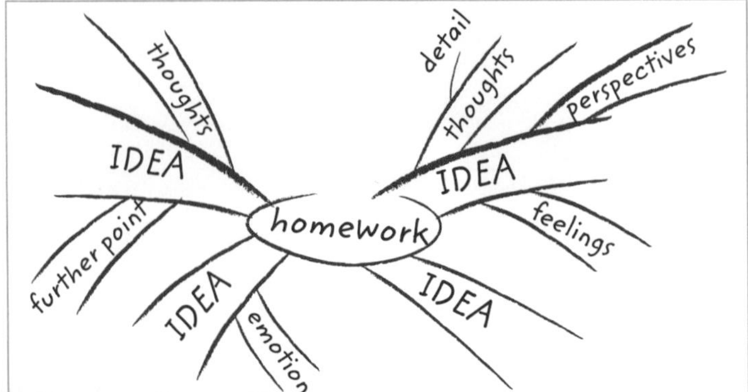

Activity 2

Look back at the task in Activity 1.

1 Try out the strategy that you think will help you to generate the most ideas quickly.

2 Evaluate how well the strategy helped you to generate ideas for the task.

Good writers often take an idea and present it in a slightly unusual way. One approach to a task would be to think about how most people would respond and then think of how you might do it differently. This approach will challenge you to express your ideas in an interesting way.

Activity 3

1 Go back to your planning notes from Activity 2. How could you express your ideas in an effective and engaging way?

Activity 4

Look at the following three tasks.

A: Write the text for a leaflet in which you inform 14-to 16-year-olds about places they could visit near you.

B: Write a blog for your school website in which you comment on the events that have taken place in your school over the past year.

C: Write an article for the school newspaper in which you explain how students feel in the time leading up to examinations.

1 For each task:
   a) Use a different strategy to note down quickly ideas that you could write about.
   b) Evaluate the ideas you have come up with. Are your ideas imaginative and interesting?

2 When you have completed these steps for all three tasks, evaluate which strategy you felt worked best for you under time pressure. This is the strategy you might develop for use in the examination.

ResultsPlus
Watch out!

You only have a short amount of time in the examination to plan your answer – probably no more than 5-10 minutes

6 Planning

This lesson will help you to...

→ **organise your ideas into a clear and effective structure**

When you read the writing task in the examination, use the strategies you have learned to plan your response quickly. A good approach is to write notes on the examination paper, labelling the task. You can refer back to them as you write and keep your writing style on track. Look at this example:

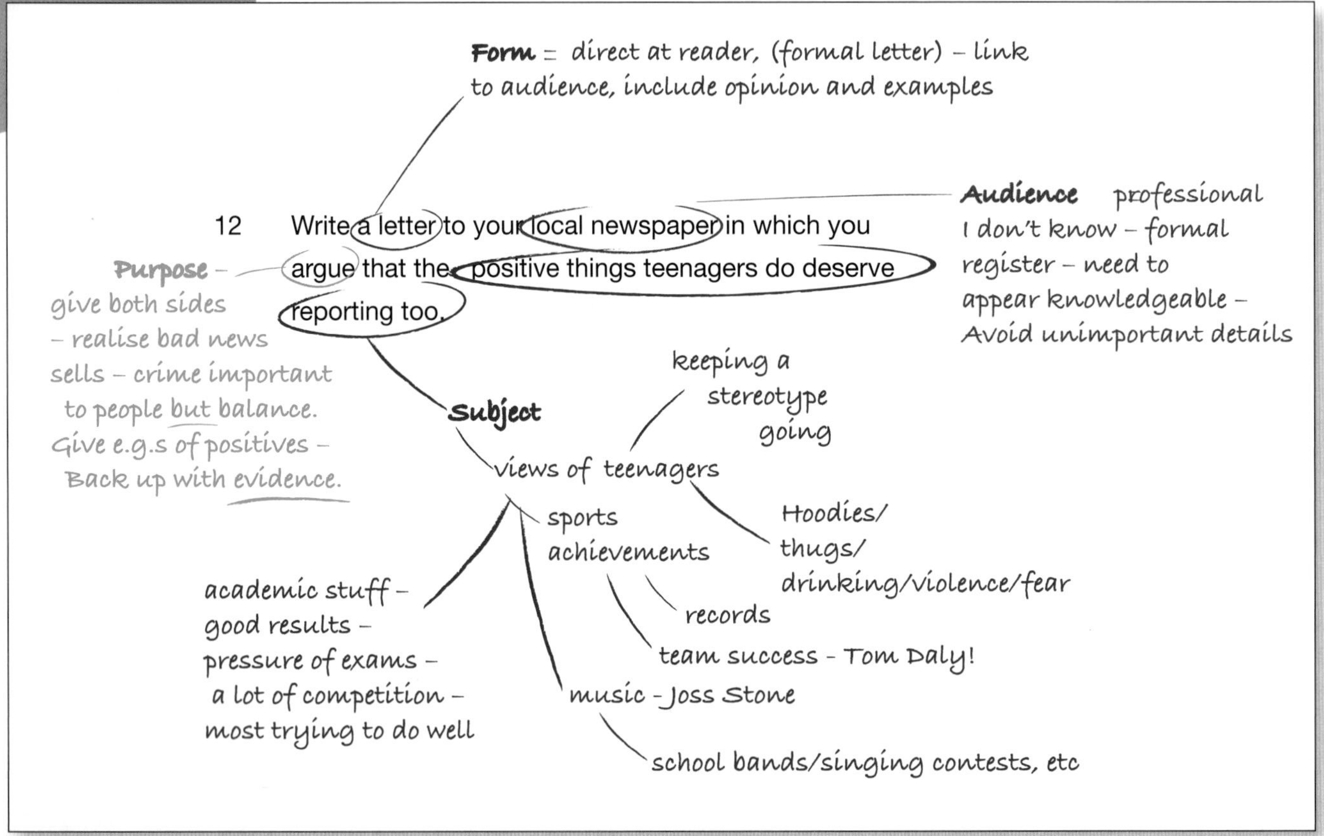

ResultsPlus
Exam tip

If you are interested in your ideas then your examiner will be too. Select the question that focuses on a topic you find interesting.

Activity 1

Using the strategies you have learned, annotate each of the following writing tasks as shown in the example above. Remember you need to plan quickly, your time in the examination is precious!

A: Write the text for a leaflet in which you try to persuade residents not to be concerned about extended opening hours at a local youth club.

B: Write an article for the school newspaper in which you describe life in your town for people of your age.

The next step is to plan your route through the writing. To do this you need to produce a paragraph map, in which you give each paragraph a title and then use bullet points to list the points that you will cover in each paragraph. You should list the points in the order in which you will use them in your writing.

You also need to decide how to organise your writing. You could use a chronological (time) order, a 'for and against' structure or you could present a different idea in each paragraph. The purpose of the text should help you decide which approach is most suitable.

Activity 2

Look at this task.

> **Write an article for the school newspaper in which you describe life in your town for people of your age.**

1 Create a paragraph plan for a response to this task. You need to:

- decide how to organise your writing
- think of titles that show what each paragraph will be about
- use bullet points to list the ideas that would be included in each paragraph.

It is important that you practise enough so that you can complete the planning process quickly, including annotating the task, generating ideas and writing a paragraph map..

Activity 3

1 Practise writing a paragraph map for Task A in Activity 1, under time pressure.

2 Practise labelling the following task and then plan a response:

> **Write the text for a speech to the school council in which you review the after-school activities on offer in your school.**

ResultsPlus
Exam Tip

In your examination, use between 10% and 20% of the time available thinking, planning and checking. Use the remaining 80%-90% writing your answer.

7 Effective openings

This lesson will help you to...

→ begin your writing clearly and effectively

There are many strategies that you can use to make the opening to your writing effective. These include using questions, making a controversial statement, making a humorous comment or bluntly stating what your point is. Look at this table which illustrates what each of these openings could look like in response to a task asking you to argue that the positive things that teenagers do deserve reporting.

Question	Why do you insist on portraying all teenagers as criminals?
Controversial	It isn't the teenagers who are committing crimes; last year only 3 people under the age of 20 were arrested in this town, but 424 people over the age of 20 years old were arrested.
Humorous	I am 15 years old and I can write; I assume that surprises you.
Blunt	I am writing to argue that you do not portray teenagers in a positive light.

These strategies will not be effective for all tasks you will be given. Your opening needs to suit the audience, purpose and form.

Activity 1

1 Use either the humorous or controversial strategy to write an opening paragraph in response to the following task:

> **Write an email to your friend in which you argue that the positive things teenagers do deserve reporting too.**

2 Which technique do you think is more effective? Why?

The opening paragraph needs to hook the audience and convince them it will be worth reading on, so you need to consider carefully the rest of your first paragraph.

Look at the use of questions in the opening paragraph of a letter to a local newspaper about the positive things teenagers do below.

> Why am I assumed to be anti-social, under-educated and violent? When I am stood on street corners with my friends, why do people give enough space for a herd of stampeding bison to pass between us? I am 15 years old, a child, a school kid. What has led to this point when people assume I am a criminal? I wonder if you feel you have a part to play.

Opens with a controversial and challenging question.

A pattern of three. Appeals to the reader's emotions.

The use of a second question creates a strong tone of voice and makes the reader think.

The final sentence prepares the reader for what the rest of the letter is about.

Activity 2

1 Write an alternative opening paragraph for this letter which has a 'blunt' opening sentence. Write the rest of the paragraph, building to a point where you can state what the letter will be about.

Being able to reread and evaluate your own writing is an important skill when writing in an examination. Using a series of questions is effective because it challenges the reader to think about the subject and their opinions on it. However, an examiner may feel the series of questions to be too aggressive for the audience, so you might want to consider changing one of the questions to a statement.

Activity 3

Look at this task:

> **Write a speech for the school assembly on Leavers' Day in which you review the time you spent at the school.**

1. **Write four different opening sentences using one of the strategies given below in each one. Give yourself no more than one minute to write each opening sentence.**
   - question
   - controversial
   - statement
   - humorous
   - blunt
2. **Briefly review the four sentences. Ask yourself whether it is suitable for the audience and purpose, whether it hooks the reader in and whether it introduces the point of the writing.**
3. **Choose which of the sentences you would use in your examination. Explain your choice.**
4. **Use the sentence you have chosen to draft an opening paragraph for the task.**

The opening paragraph is sometimes the most difficult to write. Practising getting started quickly will ensure that you do not freeze in the examination room.

Activity 4

Look at the following two tasks:

> **A: Write an email to a web forum on the subject of underage drinking.**

> **B: Write a blog in which you comment on the events that have taken place in your school over the past year.**

1. **For each task write an opening sentence using each of the strategies you have learned.**
2. **Evaluate the openings you have written, asking yourself if they grab the reader's attention and are suitable for the audience and purpose you are writing for**
3. **Choose the opening you feel works best and use it to draft the opening paragraph of the response.**

8 Linking paragraphs

This lesson will help you to...

- → link sentences in your writing
- → structure your writing effectively

When writing you need to take lots of separate ideas on a subject and organise them into the best order to respond to your task. You need to be able to build strong paragraphs and put them into a logical sequence so that the whole piece of writing flows.

A strong way to begin a paragraph is to use a **topic sentence**. This will indicate the idea that is the subject of the paragraph. The topic sentence in this paragraph clearly indicates that the paragraph is going to be about the debate surrounding the length of the school holidays.

> **There's always a debate every year at this time about whether school holidays are too long or too short.** Teachers and students are the first to shout that they could do with more time off whilst parents and some theorists think that children should get back into the classroom. But who is right?

Topic sentence

Activity 1

Look at the following task:

> A: Write a newspaper article arguing that school holidays are too long or too short.

Write four topic sentences that you could use for different paragraphs in a response to this task. Use the subjects given below for each paragraph in the order you feel is best:

- **length**
- **activities**
- **location**
- **returning to school.**

To link ideas within a paragraph you can use **cohesive devices** – language features that connect the text. For example: a writer can use a topic sentence to help introduce a paragraph; use a connective to show where the writing is going next such as, 'However,' or use the words from the title to keep the reader focused on the topic. Look at the following paragraphs continuing the debate on school holidays:

> Those that think school holidays are too long argue that it takes the students a while to get back in the learning mode after the break. There is evidence to suggest that students dip at the start of each year and take a little time to progress further than they were before. Therefore, the sooner they get back into 'learning mode,' the sooner they can begin achieving again.
>
> However, those who think holidays are too short think that it's good for students to have a long break to refresh themselves and to learn to have fun. Although parents may feel holidays are wasted time that could be used for learning, they give children time to explore their imagination and to work out for themselves how they like to spend their time.

Synonyms.

Discourse markers.

Topic sentence indicates the subject of the paragraph.

Reinforcement of key words or phrases through repetition.

Topic sentence.

Activity 2

Look back to your response to Activity 1.

1 **Did you use any cohesive devices? Identify the cohesive devices you used and say how they improved your writing.**

2 **Adapt your response to include at least one example of each reinforcement device and at least one discourse marker per paragraph.**

Another way of making your writing cohesive is to refer back to ideas in the previous paragraph. Look at the opening two paragraphs of this piece of writing.

Why do you insist on portraying all teenagers as criminals? When I open the newspaper I read about teenage mums, teenage knife crime, teenage drop-out rates, teenage unemployment. I know that my grandparents are worried to walk through the city centre on a Saturday because they believe that groups of teenagers will attack them.

The image of hooligan and yob really does not work when you start to look closely at the achievements of the teenagers in your community. The majority of students compete hard and enjoy success, especially on the sports field.

The opening paragraph builds the point that teenagers are being represented badly. The second paragraph repeats this idea and the opening sentence makes it clear that this paragraph is going to focus on why this is wrong.

Activity 3

Here are possible topic sentences for paragraphs 3 and 4:

Paragraph 3: Students can play music.

Paragraph 4: There is so much pressure on teenagers to achieve.

1 **Rewrite these topic sentences so that they build more effectively on the ideas in the previous paragraphs.**

A final way to link paragraphs effectively is to end a paragraph with a question to set up the issues that will be addressed in the next.

2 **Add a question that links paragraph 2 on the sporting achievements of teenagers to the subject of paragraph 3.**

Opening paragraphs often introduce the issues and give some brief background details that will be explored in later paragraphs. Closing paragraphs often summarise the main points or give an overview of what has been said. This helps to create a cohesive text as shown in these opening and closing paragraphs from giving advice to parents of a child who refuses to go to school.

Opening paragraph

Your daughter's behaviour sounds like school refusal (SR) – this is a known disorder. One in four children occasionally refuses to attend school, and it becomes a routine problem in about 2 per cent of children. It is seen equally in boys and girls and generally occurs between the ages of 5 and 11 (due to school transitions), and 14 and 15 (due to puberty and associated pressures). Most children with SR will have shown related difficulties at some earlier time – separation anxiety when first going to school, social anxiety, or low mood.

Concluding paragraph

As parents, you need to not be anxious with your daughter. You are her role models, and unless there really is something bad going on at school, you can show her how to face fear in life. The best outcomes are seen when families become assertive and organised in the face of their child's chaotic behaviour.

Notice how the opening paragraph gives background details on school refusal. The concluding paragraph gives overall advice to the parents about how they should deal with the problem.

Activity 4

Write an opening and concluding paragraph to a text that gives advice to parents of children who feel under pressure because of examinations, and who are possibly working too hard on their studies.

To make sure you can link paragraphs effectively and give a sense of the whole text in the examination you need to practise.

Activity 5

Write a five-paragraph response to the following task:

Write a magazine article on the pros and cons of living in the city rather than the countryside.

1 Decide on the subject matter for each of the paragraphs. Remember: paragraph 1 will be your introduction and paragraph 5 will be your conclusion.

2 Write a topic sentence for the start of each paragraph.

3 Include a discourse marker in these topic sentences to show how the paragraph moves on from the previous one.

4 Complete your paragraphs, including one that uses a question that will set up the topic for the next paragraph.

Here is an example of an examination question you could be expected to answer. You will be expected to write a letter with paragraphs that link together effectively.

> Write a letter to students in which you persuade them that a trip in term time would be a good idea or would not be a good idea.
>
> (24 marks)

Activity 6

Write the letter to students. Focus on how well you link the paragraphs together.

You should spend 20 minutes on this task.

ResultsPlus
Self assessment

Before you complete this self-assessment activity, you might like to read some sample answers to this task on the following pages (100-101).

1 Check your answer to Activity 6:
- Does your opening sentence clearly introduce what the paragraph is about?
- Is there an obvious progression of your ideas between one paragraph and another?
- Is there an obvious progression of your ideas between one paragraph and another?
- Do you use discourse markers to help link the paragraphs together?

2 Now try to grade your answer to Activity 6 by applying the mark scheme opposite. You will need to be careful and precise in your marking.

■ **Higher Tier Band 1**
- text structure is generally clearly organised
- text has an opening and development
- paragraphing is broadly appropriate but some may be unlinked

● **Higher Tier Band 2**
- text structure is clearly organised
- text has an opening, development and closure
- paragraphing is controlled and successfully uses cohesive devices

▲ **Higher Tier Band 3**
- text structure is securely organised and well-judged
- effective use of coherent devices between and within paragraphs

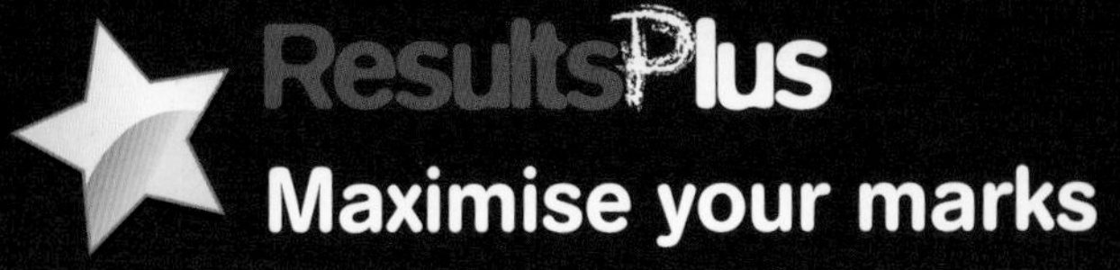

Write two paragraphs for the letter to students in which you persuade them that a trip in term time would be a good idea or would not be a good idea. You should focus on the linking of paragraphs.

Here are three student answers to the speech task on page 99. Read the answers together with the examiner comments around and after the answers. Then complete the activity.

Student 1 – Extract typical of a grade D answer

Some may argue with me that taking time out of a term to go abroad is nothing but an upset as it takes time out of the curriculum to go and enjoy yourself well. Well they are wrong because we have tried this scheme in other schools in your area and the success rates in GCSE were a big improvement, as before they averaged at 20 – 30% but now they are achieving 60 – 75% achieving A - C.*

The advantages of travelling abroad in school time is that students get to see what travelling abroad is like. They get to know what to do at the airport and what to do when booking a hotel. Pupils get to travel round the resorts on their own and can find things.

Opening sentence introduces what the paragraph is about.

Although on the same topic as the previous paragraph, this is a completely new idea that isn't linked to the first paragraph.

Examiner summary

This part of the answer is typical of grade D performance. There is some sense that the structure is clear because the student has used a sentence at the beginning of each paragraph that links to the topic of the letter. However, there is no real connection between the two paragraphs – the only link is that both paragraphs develop an idea on a similar topic.

Student 2 – Extract typical of a grade C answer

Opening sentence clearly focuses on the topic of the letter.

Having school trips in term time can have an effect on pupils because it means that they will not be attending school and this will affect their attendance. 75% of children who have low attendance in school on average do not get good results in their GCSEs than pupils who have good attendance. Mr Whitehead of OfSted said, "it is essential that children get to school as much as they can to get the best results possible."

Also, travelling to a foreign country could be bad because pupils in the class with their friends may act the clown and show off. Over the last 5 years schools trips that went abroad have had a 50% increase in violence than school trips that stayed in England.

Use of a discourse marker shows this is an further idea why travelling abroad is a bad idea.

Examiner summary

This part of the answer is typical of grade C performance. The student has used an opening sentence that links to the topic of the letter. This gives the writing a clear sense of structure. The use of the discourse marker 'Also' helps to link the paragraphs and gives the reader an understanding that the second paragraph offers another suggestion as to why school travel during term time is a bad idea.

Student 3 – Extract typical of a grade (B) answer

Good priority to this idea – this shows that the writer has an idea of the whole text as they have clearly thought about how this paragraph will link to the others.

Use of similar paragraph opening to show links between the paragraphs.

Good use of discourse markers within paragraphs.

The main reason for a trip abroad is to be with your friends and have a good time whilst you are away. You will have an informal relationship with the dedicated staff and other pupils. I was once told that because you see these people in a new light it opens up the possibility of new ideas and new possibilities. Therefore, travel abroad will make you more and more tolerant to the ideas and friendship of others.

Another reason for a trip abroad is the chance to learn. The trip will be educational therefore you will get a lot out of it. For instance, if you travel to places like France and Belgium you may want to visit the World War graves. This would be useful for a younger generation, as it will teach them the great sacrifices that the soldiers made for us to be free.

Examiner summary

This part of the answer is typical of grade B performance. The use of the phrase 'The main reason' persuades the reader that Student 3 has an idea what the whole of the text will be. This means that the structure of the writing will feel secure. The use of the phrase 'Another reason' is effective as the reader knows that each paragraph will offer reasons to support travel abroad. The use of the word 'therefore' within the paragraphs shows the student can use discourse markers within paragraphs, linking ideas throughout.

ResultsPlus
Build better answers

Move from a Grade (D) to Grade (C)

In this part of your task you need to link paragraphs using topic sentences and discourse markers. Student 1 has linked ideas at the beginning of the paragraphs to the topic of the letter. Therefore, the response appears to be clearly structured. Student 2 used a discourse marker between paragraphs to show how one topic links to the next.

Move from a Grade (C) to Grade (B)

In this part of your task you need to make it clear how the whole piece of writing is going to work. Student 3 helps the reader to understand how the first paragraph fits within the whole piece of writing. The use of the phrase 'Another reason' connects the paragraphs and the use of discourse markers within paragraphs connects ideas. There is some sense that the whole piece of writing connects together.

Putting it into Practice

1. **Explain to a partner how to link paragraphs in a piece of writing. Use as few words as possible in your explanation.**
2. **Draw a diagram that will help you to remember how to link paragraphs in a piece of writing.**

9 Choosing vocabulary

This lesson will help you to...

→ select appropriate vocabulary that makes your writing clear, precise and effective

When writing in the examination it is important to make sure you use precise vocabulary. This often means thinking about whether there is one word that can do the job of many words in a sentence. For instance:

There are many times that teenagers will behave thoughtlessly and stupidly, but there is a lot that they do not know about yet.

could be replaced with:

Often teenagers will behave immaturely but they still have a lot to learn.

Activity 1

Rewrite the following text more precisely by replacing each underlined phrase with one word:

> There are athletes who train each day to make sure that they run much quicker or jump higher or leap further. They work really hard for their own sense of achievement and to make their friends and family proud. The powerful emotion they feel makes them really push themselves more than anyone expects of them.

You also need to check that you have selected words that are effective and suitable for the task. There are usually many words that are adequate, but some are better than others in different situations. When describing a 100 metres athlete you might choose the word 'running' when writing to inform, but you might use 'sprinting' when writing to report or review.

Activity 2

Under time pressure in the examination, verbs may be the easiest words to change.

1 Read this paragraph about the examination pressure teenagers feel. Rewrite the paragraph using stronger verbs that create a more effective description.

> As the next generation of this country we work to get the results needed to move us towards our futures. We do not sit by and wait for a job to be given to us. We understand what it takes to get where we want to be. There is no final push at the end of Year 11; exams happen throughout Years 10 and 11. The pressure is constant. Is there any sympathy given for this?

Using descriptive words, such as adjectives, can give the reader a better sense of the emotions you are trying to express. They can also help the reader to see images better or understand more clearly the strength of opinion that you hold, so they are particularly useful in writing to argue or persuade. For instance:

Laura Robson is an example of a teenager who can achieve success.

could be replaced with:

Talented Laura Robson is an excellent example of a polite, modest teenager who can achieve great success.

However, overuse of adjectives and adverbs may mean you haven't selected the most precise verb or phrase. Make sure your writing is as concise as it can be, and use descriptive words only where they help the reader to understand your point better.

Activity 3

Look again at the paragraph in Activity 2 about examination pressure.

1 **Rewrite the paragraph, adding adjectives and adverbs to express the extent of the effort put in by teenagers.**

2 **Check your paragraph. Have you included adverbs and adjectives only where they help the reader to understand your point better?**

You had to practise your routine for planning and starting a piece of writing. The same practice is needed in checking your vocabulary.

Activity 4

Look at the following task:

Write an article for an information guide recommending a local attraction that might be suitable for families.

1 **Write a paragraph of your response to this task. You should:**

- **give yourself no more than eight minutes to write the paragraph**
- **check that the words you have selected are accurate and precise**
- **check that you have selected effective verbs**
- **check that you have included adjectives and adverbs in appropriate, places.**

ResultsPlus
Build better answers

Look at this examination question:

Write a letter to your teacher advising them on the right approach to bullying.

■ A Higher Tier Band 1 answer **will include words that are well chosen**, such as 'hurtful' or 'upsetting'.

● A Higher Tier Band 2 answer **will use words that are interesting and appropriate to the audience and purpose** given in the task, such as 'victimised' or 'sensitive'.

▲ A Higher Tier Band 3 answer **will include an extensive vocabulary, using words that are appropriate**, from selecting something as simple as 'wrong' to something powerful such as 'dehumanising', depending on the place it is used.

10 Selecting punctuation

This lesson will help you to...

- → use punctuation accurately
- → select punctuation for emphasis and effect

Like vocabulary, punctuation can be used to make writing more effective. Using a question mark rather than a full stop, for instance, can give the reader the feeling they have a choice. Selecting an exclamation mark can add emotion or emphasise the importance of an idea.

The first step is to make sure that you can use punctuation accurately so that your writing makes sense.

Activity 1

Look at the extract below from a letter to a newspaper that argues that the positive things that teenagers do deserve to be publicised.

> I quote Local thug 15 hits the elderly What is happening to our teenagers It is headlines like these that have prompted me to write to you It seems to me that you have taken one story and blown it out of all proportion and decided that all teenagers can be labelled because of one Local thug Is this fair You portray us as beer swigging swearing violent scavengers Have you looked closer Have you bothered to see if the news you are reporting is balanced and fair I challenge you to take another look at what is going on with teenagers today I think you will be pleasantly surprised

1 Rewrite the extract, using the correct punctuation from the marks available to you:

, . : ; ‘ ? ! ( ) “ ” – ...

In the examination, try to show that you can use a variety of punctuation marks. Don't use punctuation marks just for the sake of it, but you should check to see if you have missed any opportunities to use a wider range.

Activity 2

1 The paragraph below has accurate punctuation but it uses only full stops. Rewrite the paragraph using at least three different punctuation marks.

> Joss Stone is a good example of a teenager who achieved amazing things. She was 16 years old when she began having massive hits. Musical talent is not limited to older people. Many famous musicians started making music when they were very young. The powerful emotions that teenagers feel are often helpful in creating songs with passion. I am sure you can remember the overwhelming impact hormones can have on your creativity.

2 Write a paragraph about a young person you admire. Try to include at least three different punctuation marks.

Punctuation can also affect the way that a reader responds to a text. For instance, look at this paragraph about being a teenager:

> Adolescence and puberty can be a challenging time for anyone to cope with. Many changes happen in the body and in the way we experience emotions. This section looks at some of the changes that will take place and considers ways to help us feel good about ourselves. When these changes begin, it's easy to feel that they are only happening to you and nobody else has ever gone through this. You may find some of the physical changes worrying, or get sudden mood swings – feeling happy one moment and fed up the next, and for no apparent reason. The important thing is to realise that this is normal and that others will be experiencing similar feelings, even if they don't admit it.

Notice how changing the paragraph to using an exclamation mark and ellipses in place of full stops makes the extract feel more informal and light-hearted:

> You get sudden mood swings – feeling happy one moment and fed up the next, and for no apparent reason! The important thing is to realise that this is normal and that others will be experiencing similar feelings, even if they don't admit it...

Activity 3

Select sentences from the longer extract above on adolescence to edit to achieve the following effects:

1. **Change the punctuation of a sentence so that it expresses powerful emotions.**
2. **Change the punctuation of a sentence so that it gives the impression that you know a lot about the subject.**

You should also ensure that the punctuation choices you make are appropriate to the purpose of the text. The following text is informing the reader about Miley Cyrus. The writer has used punctuation that helps to give the reader details as clearly as possible.

Dashes act like brackets to allow the writer to insert the additional information.

Commas break up the sentence, making the meaning clear and allowing the reader to draw breath.

> Born November 23, 1992, in Nashville, Miley grew up watching her father – country superstar/ actor Billy Ray Cyrus – perform. Soon enough she caught the acting bug herself. After gaining experience as an extra in her dad's television projects, Miley acted opposite him in a recurring role on his television series, "Doc". She then went on to appear in the Tim Burton film, "Big Fish." When a 12-year-old Miley first auditioned for the title role of the Disney Channel's "Hannah Montana", she was considered too young for the part, but that didn't stop her from pressing ahead. Two years later Miley won the part she had worked so hard for, and her rise to fame began.

Simple sentence helps pass on information clearly.

Speech marks to show that this is the title of a film.

Activity 4

1. **Rewrite the paragraph on Miley Cyrus to persuade people that the young actress has had an amazing life so far. Try including question marks and exclamation marks but don't over do it!**
2. **Edit the paragraph you wrote in Activity 2 about the young person you admire. Include punctuation that will either persuade the reader, or explain your opinion.**

11 Checking and editing

This lesson will help you to...

→ **check that your work is accurate and effective.**

Checking your work is different from editing. Editing is the work done to improve choices, such as vocabulary and punctuation. Checking your work means looking for inaccuracies and then putting any mistakes right.

Making even small changes can have a big impact on what you have written. For example, look at how many errors there are in the following text:

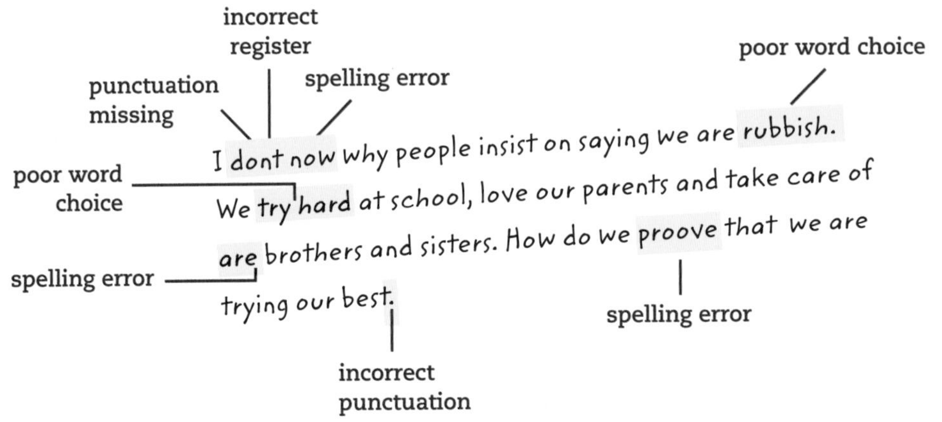

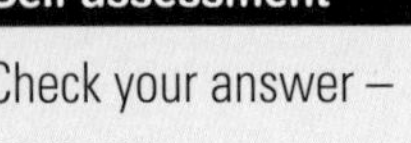

ResultsPlus
Self assessment

Check your answer – have you:

- ensured that you have answered the task you have been set?
- checked that you have corrected the spelling and punctuation mistakes you have made whilst writing in a hurry?
- changed words so you have used more effective vocabulary choices?
- made sure there are a variety of sentences in your work?

Both editing and checking should be done as you write. Stop after every paragraph and read your work back critically and make it better. Here is a checklist of things to think about:

✔ Is my writing appropriate for the purpose, audience and form?
✔ Do I stay on the subject mentioned in the task?
✔ Is my spelling correct? Do I need to try again?
✔ Do the words I have chosen make sense? Are they effective?
✔ Is my punctuation accurate? Does it make the meaning clear?
✔ Have I used a variety of sentences?
✔ Do my sentences make sense?
✔ Do my paragraphs flow logically? Have I changed paragraph when I have changed topic?

Activity 1

1 **Rewrite the paragraph above. Make changes to remove the problems highlighted and improve the quality of the writing.**

When you are in an examination, time is limited, so you need to learn to check and edit quickly. You may not have time to edit as much as you would like, so focus on checking and correcting errors where necessary.

Activity 2

Choose two responses to tasks you have written in previous lessons.

1 For the first response, read through your work, checking and editing what you have written. Cross out and change anything that you think could be better.

2 For the second response, check and edit your work, focusing on correcting any obvious errors and ensuring you have responded to the task's form, audience and purpose.

ResultsPlus
Watch out!

There may be little point in checking your work in the last five minutes if you have completely misunderstood the task. Write a paragraph and then check your work. Write another paragraph and read back through again! The final five minutes should merely be for tweaking the odd word or phrasing.

Assessment Practice

Here is an example of an examination question you could be expected to answer.

As part of this question you will be expected to check and edit your work, making the best possible choices.

Write a letter to students in which you persuade them that a trip in term time would be a good idea or would not be a good idea.

(24 marks)

Activity 3

Write a paragraph for the letter to students. Focus on how well you check and edit your work to make the best possible choices.

You should spend 10 minutes on this task.

ResultsPlus
Self assessment

Before you complete this self-assessment activity, you might like to read some sample answers to this task on the following pages (108-109).

1 **Check your answer to Activity 3:**
- Have you checked your spelling?
- Have you made sure you use a variety of words and punctuation?
- Have you varied the sentences you have used and have you written these sentences accurately?

2 **Now try to grade your answer to Activity 3 by applying the mark scheme opposite. You will need to be careful and precise in your marking.**

Higher Tier Band 1
- spelling is mostly accurate, with some slips which do not hinder meaning
- generally sound use of punctuation, mostly helping create intended effects
- sentences are generally clearly structured

Higher Tier Band 2
- spelling is almost always accurate
- sound use of full range of punctuation, helping intended effects to be created
- some variety in sentences that are clearly structured

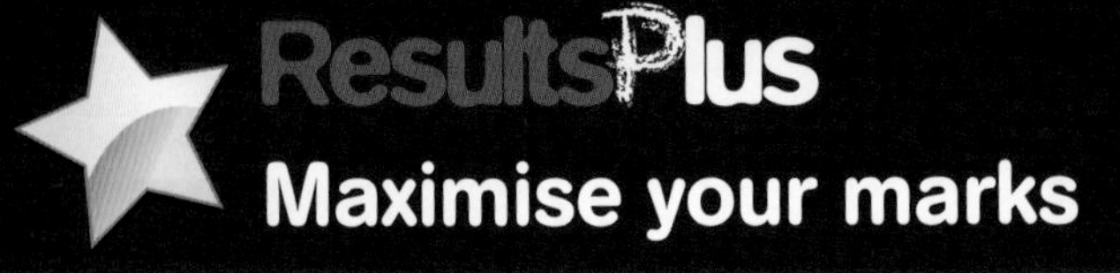

Maximise your marks

Write a letter to students in which you persuade them that a trip in term time would be a good idea or would not be a good idea.

Write a paragraph for the letter to students. Focus on how well you check and edit your work to make the best possible choices.

Here are three student answers to the letter task on page 107. Read the answers together with the examiner comments around and after the answers. Then complete the activity.

Student 1 – Extract typical of a grade (D) answer

Attempting to use a variety of sentences. However, this is a run-on sentence and needed splitting into two different sentences.

Another point is that if you take a trip abroad there is a big chance that you may lose one of the pupils or one of them may run away and in a country which the language is different that could be life threatening. In the last 3 years over 1000 children aged 12 – 16 have gone missing in Spain on school trips and family holidays. Head of the directgov website Mr Baldwin said "It is ok taking a few people on a trip but 1 full class is not good in case you lose a pupil or members of the class bully that pupil into running away"

Accurate punctuation and apt for this piece of writing.

Spelling is accurate the vocabulary choices are quite basic.

Examiner summary

This part of the answer is typical of grade D performance. Student 1 has used mostly accurate spelling and punctuation, although the choices they have made lack ambition – this means the examiner thinks it is easier for this student to be accurate than someone who has made difficult choices. Examiners much prefer ambition than accuracy! The student has attempted to use a variety of sentences, but the opening sentence is too long. The student should have used punctuation to split this up.

Student 2 – Extract typical of a grade (C) answer

Repetition of the words 'pressure' and 'stress' – apt word choices but more variety needed.

Students should take holidays in term time to get away from the stress placed on them by teachers. Many pupils feel like their teachers put too much pressure on them to complete work in deadlines which are impossible. 78 out of 89 students thought that teachers where putting too much pressure on them and that this affected their health and confidence. Sarah Cook, a pupil in an all girl school, took a two week holiday in term time to get a brake from all the stress. She felt like this helped her to reach her deadlines because she had a better approach to her work.

Accurate sentences but no variety of punctuation used.

Some checking of homophones needed but spelling mostly accurate.

Examiner summary

This part of the answer is typical of grade C performance. Student 2's response is mostly accurate but they do need to make sure that their choice of homophones is accurate – 'where' and 'brake' are inaccurate. The vocabulary is appropriate for a formal letter about holidays, but Student 2 could have varied the words used to describe pressure and stress a little more.

Student 3 – Extract typical of a grade B answer

Use of a question for effect, challenging the reader to disagree.

If taking a holiday is good for you at that particular time, then why not take one? There are many students who are bullied in schools, so taking a break would give them time to relax without other students interfering. John Mandy, a Year 10 student from St Bernard's School in London, has been bullied for the past 2 years. In order to relieve the pressure of this abuse, he took a holiday in Majorca with his family. His father took time to talk things through with John at this time. After returning to school John found he was able to find a group of friends who accepted him.

Spelling is accurate throughout.

Controlled structure, using a variety of sentences to keep the reader interested.

Examiner summary

This part of the answer is typical of grade B performance. This student is accurate throughout and there are some sound vocabulary choices. There is a use of a question for effect and the other sentences show accurate use of a variety of sentence structures.

ResultsPlus
Build better answers

Move from a Grade D to Grade C

In this part of your task you need to make sure your work is accurate and precise. Student 1 made a number of mistakes, whereas Student 2 ensured that they were accurate. In addition, Student 2 demonstrated that they could structure sentences well. Student 1 included a greater variety of punctuation but Student 2 is more typical of C grade performance because the paragraph was clear and accurate.

Move from a Grade C to Grade B

In this part of your task you need to ensure that you have made choices that are effective as well as accurate. Student 3 managed to include a variety of punctuation and accurate word choices. As with Student 2, Student 3's response is clear and accurate but includes more variety. It is the control and the effect of these varied choices that mean the student can achieve a B grade. The student has clearly thought about how they want the reader to react and has made sure they have selected, or controlled sentence choice throughout, to achieve this effect.

Putting it into Practice

1 **Look back over a paragraph that you have written in class. You should select a paragraph that was written under pressure. Check and edit the paragraph to ensure that it is accurate but also that it includes a variety of word, punctuation and sentence choices.**

Examination Practice

Examiner's tip

This is a sample of the writing section for the Unit 2 Foundation Tier Examination for GCSE English Language.

Examiner's tip

Select one of the questions to write about. Remember to make your writing appropriate for the specified purpose, form and audience.

Examiner's tip

Use the bullet points to help shape your response.

GCSE English Language
FOUNDATION TIER

SECTION B: WRITING

Answer **ONE** question in this section.

EITHER

*9 Your local council is planning some changes and has asked you to write a review of community facilities for young people.

Write a review which includes suggestions for future improvements.

In your review, you may wish to consider:

- a general introduction on existing community facilities for young people in your area
- any gaps in community facilities for young people
- affordable ideas for community facilities for young people
- why the new community facilities would be welcome
- any other ideas you may have. (24)

OR

*10 Write an article for an information guide recommending a place of interest in the UK that might be enjoyable to visit.

In your article, you may wish to consider:

- features that make the place worth visiting
- any helpful hints or tips for the visit
- any other ideas you may have. (24)

TOTAL FOR SECTION B = 24 MARKS

TOTAL FOR PAPER = 64 MARKS

GCSE English Language
HIGHER TIER

SECTION B: WRITING

Answer **ONE** question in this section.

EITHER

*9 Your local council is planning some changes and has asked you to write a review of community facilities for young people.

Write a review which includes suggestions for future improvements.

(24)

OR

*10 Write an article for an information guide recommending a place of interest in the UK that might be enjoyable to visit.

(24)

TOTAL FOR SECTION B = 24 MARKS

TOTAL FOR PAPER = 64 MARKS

Examiner's tip

This is a sample of the writing section for the Unit 2 Higher Tier Examination for GCSE English Language.

Examiner's tip

Select one of the questions to write about. Remember to make your writing appropriate for the specified purpose, form and audience.

Examiner's tip

This is a sample of the writing section for the Unit 2 Foundation Tier Examination for GCSE English.

Examiner's tip

Select one of the questions to write about. Remember to make your writing appropriate for the specified purpose, form and audience.

Examiner's tip

Use the bullet points to help shape your response.

GCSE English
FOUNDATION TIER

SECTION C: WRITING

You MUST answer EITHER Question 11 OR Question 12 in this section.

EITHER

*11 Write a magazine article for parents with the title 'What makes a good school'?

You may wish to use some of these topics to help you write your article:

- behaviour and discipline codes
- teachers
- extra curricular activities
- buildings and facilities
- other ideas you may have. (48 marks)

OR

*12 Write a speech on the topic of 'Stress and Modern Life' to be given to a group of your peers.

You may wish to include:

- what you mean by stress
- the main causes of stress for young people
- positive suggestions on how young people can cope with stress
- any other aspects of the topic. (48 marks)

TOTAL FOR SECTION B = 48 MARKS

TOTAL FOR PAPER = 96 MARKS

GCSE English
HIGHER TIER

SECTION C: WRITING

You MUST answer EITHER Question 11 OR Question 12 in this section.

EITHER

*11 Write a magazine article for parents with the title 'What makes a good school'?

(48 marks)

OR

*12 Write a speech on the topic of 'Stress and Modern Life' to be given to a group of your peers.

(48 marks)

TOTAL FOR SECTION B = 48 MARKS

TOTAL FOR PAPER = 96 MARKS

Examiner's tip

This is a sample of the writing section for the Unit 2 Higher Tier Examination for GCSE English.

Examiner's tip

Select one of the questions to write about. Remember to make your writing appropriate for the specified purpose, form and audience.

Unit 3 Creative English: Writing

This unit is a GCSE English unit. If you are taking GCSE English Language, turn to page 144 for Unit 3: Spoken Language.

The Creative English unit gives you the opportunity to develop your speaking and listening skills, study a selection of poems and to produce your own piece of creative writing. This student book unit focuses on the creative writing task and helps you to develop your creative writing skills. You will read different examples of fiction writing – narratives, descriptions, monologues and scripts and learn how to produce your own creative writing in response to a piece of stimulus material which you'll be given to spark ideas for your writing. There are lots of different stimulus materials and activities in this section of the book for you to practise with. You will see how professional writers create effective fiction writing and try to use similar techniques in your own writing. The texts and activities you will encounter as you develop these skills are all focused on helping you to achieve the best grade you can in your Unit 3 controlled assessment task.

Your assessment

This unit is a controlled assessment unit for GCSE English. You will complete **one** Creative Writing task which you will have two hours to complete. The task will be based on one of four themes: *Relationships, Clashes and Collisions, Somewhere, Anywhere*, or *Taking a Stand*. You will be given stimulus material based on the chosen theme (this could be an image, podcast or video clip) and asked to write a narrative, description, monologue or script in response to a task. You can write up to 1000 words in your response.

Your response to the task must show that you can:

- ✔ write clearly, effectively and imaginatively in a specific form to engage your reader
- ✔ make sure that you spell, punctuate and use grammar accurately and appropriately for the purpose of your writing and to achieve the desired effect.

Assessment Objectives

Your response to the writing task will be marked using these Assessment Objectives:

- ✔ Write clearly, effectively and imaginatively, using and adapting forms and selecting vocabulary appropriate to the task and purpose in ways that engage the reader.
- ✔ Organise information and ideas into structured and sequenced sentences, paragraphs and whole texts, using a variety of linguistic and structural features to support cohesion and overall coherence.
- ✔ Use a range of sentence structures for clarity, purpose and effect, with accurate punctuation and spelling.

This student book unit will help you to understand what these require you to do so that you can write a successful response to your controlled assessment writing task.

1 Generating ideas

This lesson will help you to...

→ **use stimuli to generate ideas to include in your writing**

For your controlled assessment creative writing task, you will be asked to write 1000 words in the form of a narrative, description, monologue or script. You will be given a piece of stimulus material to generate ideas. This material could be a photograph, a video, or a podcast, for example.

By answering a series of questions about your response to the stimulus material you can generate engaging ideas for your writing. It is often best not to focus on one idea too quickly. You should write down the first things that come into your head before developing any of these ideas in more detail.

Activity 1

Here is a picture similar to one that you could be given as a stimulus for writing.

1 Look at the picture and write down your answers to these questions.
   - What is the first thing you focus on?
   - What do you focus on next?
   - Where do you think the place is?
   - Who do you think goes there?
   - Why do they go there?
   - Would you go there?
   - What does the image remind you of?
   - What do you think its name is?
   - What has happened?
   - Who was involved?
2 Reread your answers to the questions. List the ideas that you like and decide how they could link together to form a piece of creative writing.
3 Decide how you want to present your ideas in response to to this stimulus: narrative, description, monologue or script.
4 In 150 words, summarise the idea that you have come up with from the picture.

Another strategy to generate ideas for your creative writing controlled assessment task is to look at any characters in the stimulus material and think about their stories and **perspective** on events.

Activity 2

Here is another picture that you could use as a stimulus for writing. Study this photo of a lioness and her cubs.

1 **Write a summary of a story from the different characters' perspectives. You should:**

   a) **include details from before and after the moment captured**
   b) **consider the thoughts and feelings of the characters involved.**

Sometimes it is useful to imagine the thoughts and feelings of other characters who are not the central focus of the stimulus.

2 **Write a paragraph to tell the story from the cubs' perspectives. Imagine what their thoughts and feelings would be.**

3 **Reread your notes. Decide which character in the stimulus offers the best story for a narrative, description, monologue or script.**

ResultsPlus
Watch out!

Don't make your ideas too big. Simple is best. You don't get marks for the complexity of your story; you achieve marks for how well you write. Think of simple ideas or situations and then write in a way that shows you can control complex language

Most writers advise against rejecting any idea until it is written on the page. It is very easy to block the flow of ideas by trying hard to be intelligent and original while the page is still blank.

If you do hit a mental block a good activity is to close your eyes and listen for the sounds you can hear in the place where your creative writing is set. List the sounds on a piece of paper. Then try to write a paragraph that could explain the noises. This is especially effective if you choose a completely different setting, like a dark lane, or a busy marketplace.

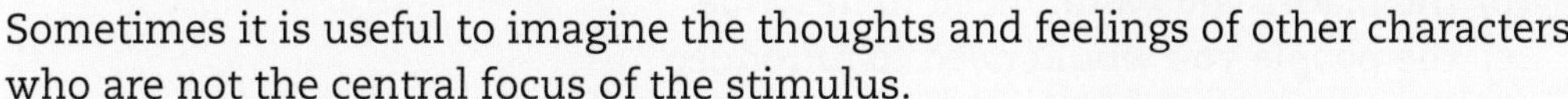

Activity 3

1 **Look at the stimulus material you have been given for your controlled assessment task. Try out the strategy outlined above.**

ResultsPlus
Self assessment

Check your answer – have you:
- generated an idea that will grab your readers' attention?
- thought through the idea so that you can develop characters/descriptons/ events effectively?
- used a variety of planning techniques to make sure you have the best idea possible?

2 Narrative writing

This lesson will help you to...

→ **create interesting and imaginative narratives**

When you write a narrative you first need to decide what your story will be about. In your controlled assessment task you will receive more marks for the way you tell your story than for the story that you tell, so keep the plot simple.

Your narrative is likely to focus on an event in one person's life. You may find it easier to build your plot around something you have experienced. For example, you could watch people at a bus stop and imagine their lives!

Activity 1

Look at the stimulus material and the task you have been given for your controlled assessment creative writing task.

1 Think about how it could relate to a simple event in your life.

2 Using this event as the plot to your narrative, make notes on the following:

a) the background story the reader would need
b) the places you would need to describe
c) the people you would need to introduce
d) the events that you would need to describe
e) the reactions of the characters to the events.

Your narrative for the controlled assessment is short, so you need to establish the setting and mood quickly. A great narrative will suggest and imply the mood and setting, rather than state it. Read the opening to *The Woman in Black* by Susan Hill, below.

It was nine-thirty on Christmas Eve. As I crossed the long entrance hall of Monk's Piece on my way from the dining room, where we had just enjoyed the first of the happy, festive meals, towards the drawing room and the fire around which my family were now assembled, I paused and then, as I often do in the course of an evening, went to the front door, opened it and stepped outside.

I have always liked to take a breath of the evening, to smell the air, whether it is sweetly scented and balmy with the flowers of midsummer, pungent with the bonfires and leaf mould of autumn, or crackling cold from frost and snow. I like to look about me at the sky above my head, whether there are moon and stars or utter blackness, and into the darkness ahead of me; I like to listen for the cries of nocturnal creatures and the moaning rise and fall of the wind, or the pattering of the rain in the orchard trees, I enjoy the rush of air towards me up the hill from the flat pastures of the river valley.

Immediate sense of time and place. It allows us to think about the images of Christmas Eve we have in our minds. (It was nine-thirty on Christmas Eve.)

Creates image of a large house. (long entrance hall)

A happy Christmas – this is a warm, safe and inviting image. (enjoyed the first of the happy, festive meals … family were now assembled)

Description of the seasons using all the senses gives an impression that the book is set in the middle of the countryside. (is sweetly scented … crackling cold from frost and snow.)

The sounds of nature are all gentle, the narrator is not threatened by the world outside. (I enjoy the rush of air … river valley.)

Activity 2

1 **Using the ideas and mood in *The Woman in Black*, write your own version of the opening, changing the setting to a small flat in the middle of a city.**

2 **List the choices you made to change the setting of the narrative.**

3 **Check your paragraph. Have you successfully created your setting and mood without saying too much?**

You also need to create a character around whom the story will revolve. Use description, actions and thoughts to make your characters convincing.

In the next section of *The Woman in Black* the reader learns about the main character's appearance and personality:

appearance — personality

personality — I was then thirty-five and I had been a widower for the past twelve years. I had no taste at all for social life and, although in good general health, was prone to occasional nervous illnesses and conditions, as a result of the experiences I will come to relate. Truth to tell, I was growing old well before my time, a sombre, pale-complexioned man with a strained expression – a dull dog. — appearance

appearance — personality

Activity 3

1 **Rewrite this paragraph, changing it so the narrator is portrayed as a lively and exciting young man.**

2 **List the choices you made to change the character of the narrative.**

Activity 4

Refer back to your stimulus material and the simple plot that you decided on for your controlled assessment task in Activity 1.

1 **Name the one or two characters that will be involved in your narrative. Make notes about their personality and their appearance.**

2 **Find an image of a place that is similar to where your story will be set or select a place that you know well. Make notes about how you could describe the setting.**

3 Descriptive writing

This lesson will help you to...

→ **create interesting and imaginative descriptions**

If you are producing a piece of descriptive writing for your controlled assessment task, you first need to make sure you know exactly what you are describing. Writing a description from a memory or from a picture is easier than trying to describe something from your imagination.

First, you need to select which details you are going to describe. One way to do this is to choose key nouns that will form a structure for your description.

Activity 1

Look at the photograph of a man.

1. **Select five nouns that you think are the most important to include in a description.**
2. **Carefully select adjectives to describe the nouns you have chosen. You should then use these noun phrases to develop descriptive sentences by including a powerful verb.**
3. **Here are some noun phrases that describe details in the image. Improve these noun phrases by selecting adjectives that better describe the man.**

   a) his lined forehead **b) the round glasses** **c) a big coat**
4. **Create a noun phrase for each of the nouns you selected for your description.**
5. **Select a verb for each of the noun phrases that you have written and turn them into sentences. For example:** ***His lined cheeks were creased against the wind.***

It is important to look at objects in detail and give the reader a complete sense of the person, place or experience you are describing. You need to use all the senses of the reader to help them to feel as if they are there.

Read the following description of a city near Christmas. Notice how the writer has used the reader's sense of smell, sound and sight to capture the feeling of the shop in the morning.

SIGHT – the writer captures an image of Christmas lights.

Brightly coloured lights from windows illuminate the frosted pavements. People hurry on, placing quick feet carefully on the cobwebbed ice patterns spinning across the coarse ground. Nobody has time to look at the delicate display of angels and stars scattered deliberately amongst the shoes or clothes or toys or sweets.

SMELL – there is a mixture of smells to help the reader imagine the shopping scene.

The sweet aroma of horse chestnuts mixed with the bitterness of coffee spin out from a festive stall. Shoppers, stopping to taste the spice of mulled wine, breathe mist. Huddled close they chatter and giggle and hum as they sip at their drink.

SOUND – the different, excited sounds of the people are captured here.

Activity 2

Look at the stimulus material for your creative writing task. Make a list of words for each of the senses that will help you to describe the scene, person or experience you are going to write about.

You can also add depth and detail to descriptions by using **metaphors** and **similes**. These comparisons use the experiences and knowledge of the reader to help them picture what the writer is describing. For instance, in the extract describing Christmas shopping the writer uses the metaphor 'cobwebbed ice patterns spinning across the coarse ground' to allow the reader to see the way that the ice had formed on the ground.

ResultsPlus
Watch out!

- There is no need to tell a story when writing a description! The point is to capture a person, place or possibly a moment in time. There doesn't need to be characters and plot – just a picture painted with words.

Activity 3

Look back at the descriptive sentences you wrote about the man in Activity 1.

1. **Select two objects in the photo or features of the man and decide what they remind you of.**
2. **Describe them using a metaphor and a simile. Try to be original – don't rely on clichés.**

Now you need to put your descriptive sentences together to form a complete description. Remember, this doesn't mean telling a story as in a narrative – it doesn't need a plot. Just choose a logical order to describe the person, place or experience.

Activity 4

Revisit the stimulus material in Lesson 1 Activity 2 and write a descriptive paragraph. Remember to include:

a) **descriptive sentences built from nouns, adjectives and then verbs**
b) **descriptions that use the senses**
c) **similes and metaphors**
d) **a logical descriptive order from a consistent viewpoint.**

4 Monologues

This lesson will help you to...

→ **create interesting and imaginative monologues**

A monologue is an extended speech by one character. They are either speaking at length to the audience or directing their thoughts to another character.

Activity 1

Read the extract of a monologue below from *A Cream Cracker under the Settee* by Alan Bennett. If possible, watch a video or listen to a recording of the extract.

Doris and Wilfred. They don't get called Doris now. They don't get called Wilfred. Museum, names like that. That's what they're all called in Stafford House. Alice and Doris. Mabel and Gladys. Antiques. Keep them under lock and key. 'What's your name? Doris? Right. Pack your case. You belong in Stafford House.'

A home. Not me. No fear.

....

She closes her eyes. A pause.

I wish I was ready for bed. All washed and in a clean nightie and the bottle in, all sweet and crisp and clean like when I was little on Baking Night, sat in front of the fire with my long hair still.

Her eyes close and she sings a little to herself. The song, which she only half remembers, is My Alice Blue Gown.

Pause.

Never mind. It's done with now, anyway.

LIGHT FADES.

1 What are the differences between a monologue and a narrative you are used to reading in books?

The first step in the process of writing a monologue is to choose the character who is speaking and get to know them.

Activity 2

Choose one of the people from the images below. Make notes on:

a) what you think the character is like

b) what concerns them.

As with a narrative, the story that the character tells needs to be simple. Your monologue will recount only a brief snippet of the character's thoughts. A good approach would be to pick a moment in time when the character is having an interesting thought.

ResultsPlus
Watch out!

Be careful to remember who is speaking! It is easy to fall into telling a story rather than allowing a character to speak the thoughts they have about an event or a person.

Activity 3

1 Copy and complete the table below. Summarise the thoughts that Character 2 might have in response to the request or comments of Character 1. If you think they may react in more than one way, select the response you would find most interesting to read or write about.

Character 1	Request/ Comment	Character 2	Response
Father	What do you want to do with your life?	Son	
Husband	I still love you after all this time.	Wife	
Teacher	Can't you try any harder?	Student	

2 Refer back to your thoughts about the character you selected in Activity 2 and what would concern them.

a) Select a moment in time when they might think or voice these concerns.

b) Select another character to whom they might direct their thoughts or speech. Or do you think they would express their thoughts only to themselves/the reader?

A monologue is the voice of a character. So you need to listen to people speak and see their words written down to help you decide how to write down your character's thoughts.

Activity 4

1 Talk with three of your classmates about a general topic such as what you did at the weekend. Do you use the same language and vocabulary?

2 Refer back to your notes on your character from Activity 2. List the choices you will make about how they will speak.

5 Scripts

This lesson will help you to...

→ **write interesting and imaginative scripts**

If you choose to write a script for your controlled assessment task, you need to write effective speech, as you would in a monologue, but scripts involve more than one person speaking so you will need to create a voice for each character.

Activity 1

1 **Look at these two images. What sort of character do you think each person is? Write a paragraph about each character making up some details about their life.**

2 **How do you imagine these characters would speak? Write a short conversation in which the characters introduce themselves to each other. Think carefully about the following:**
- **would they speak formally or informally?**
- **would they include technical vocabulary or words that they use in their day to day life?**
- **would they use complete sentences?**
- **would they tell jokes?**
- **would they have a lot to say?**
- **would they be confident or hesitant?**

Effective dialogue shows what a character is like through the way they speak. You should also try to use dialogue to show the relationship between characters. Here is an exchange between Ben and Amy. Ben is a computer expert who takes life very seriously. Amy is very laid back and just wants her friend to mend her computer.

Ben: I think you'll find that the problem lies in the hard drive. You don't have enough RAM to manage the multiple programs you're running.

Amy: Rams running... where are the ewes?

Ben: No, Amy. You don't understand. RAM is memory on your computer. Programs are the applications you do your work in.

Amy: So...mm... you'll mend this sheep problem for me then?

Ben: Yes...

Complete sentences show that he takes this very seriously.

Technical vocabulary shows his expertise.

The joke shows she is really laid back.

Abrupt reply and short sentences suggest he is trying to be patient.

The hesitation suggests she doesn't understand or wasn't listening. She ignores his comment and asks for her computer to be mended.

This suggests he has given up trying to explain – it isn't abrupt so he is likely to be despairing rather than angry.

Activity 2

1 **Write a sentence describing the relationship between the two characters you created in Activity 1.**

2 **Write a brief dialogue between your two characters in which you show what their relationship is like.**

The characters and their relationship can be made much clearer through the use of stage directions, which tell the actors how to play the parts of the characters in your script. Here is the same script featuring Ben and Amy with stage directions included:

Ben: *[seriously]* I think you'll find that the problem lies in the hard drive. You don't have enough RAM to manage the multiple programs you're running.
Amy: *[still staring at the TV]* Rams running... where are the ewes?
Ben: *[standing between Amy and the TV]* No, Amy. You don't understand. RAM is memory on your computer. Programs are the applications you do your work in.
Amy: So... mm... you'll mend this sheep problem for me then?
Ben: *[rolling eyes]* Yes...

Changing the stage directions can have a big impact on the effect of a script. The personality of the characters and the relationship they share can change, as can the story being told.

Activity 3

1 Adapt the conversation between Ben and Amy by changing the stage directions. Explain the differences the different stage directions make to:

a) the personality of the characters
b) the relationship they share
c) the story being told.

2 Include stage directions in the script you created in Activity 2. Try out different stage directions to see what impact these will have.

As a script writer you also need to set the scene. These instructions will be used by the stage or set designer when your script is performed. Here are the set design instructions for the conversation between Ben and Amy.

Amy is watching TV, her feet up on a stool, hugging a cushion. Ben is at her dining room table in a different room. He is sitting upright on the edge of the chair, laptop in front of him. He has clearly created a very neat space amongst the chaos of paperwork on the table.

Activity 4

1 How do these instructions for the set design help to communicate ideas about character relationships and the story?

2 Write a paragraph in which you set the scene for the dialogue you wrote for Activities 2 and 3

6 Creating characters

This lesson will help you to...

- → create interesting and believable characters
- → understand narrative perspective

In your creative writing task it is important that you create convincing characters. A narrative may focus on the actions of a character; your descriptive writing may describe a character; monologues and scripts are the voices of characters.

You need to balance telling the reader enough about them to build a good picture and making sure you don't tell the reader too much. The reader will fill in the details themselves. Read the extract from *The Tar Man* by Linda Buckley-Archer and then read the expanded version which includes the details that the reader is meant to assume.

The expanded version is much harder to read because the additional information breaks the flow of the story.

Original

His head was cocked to one side as if straining to hear something. Satisfied that he was alone, the dark figure slumped forward and laid his cheek against the horse's neck, expelling the breath that he had been holding in. The Tar Man patted the horse's neck and wiped sweat from his brow, though every nerve and sinew was ready for a fight.

Expanded

His head was cocked to one side as if straining to hear something; he was scared that there might be someone around that he would need to fight. Satisfied that he was alone, the dark figure slumped forward, for he was tired and shocked by the events, and laid his cheek against the horse's neck, expelling the breath he had been holding in. His horse was important to him and lying against it made him feel safe enough to breathe again. He had been so terrified he had been unable to do so. The Tar Man patted the horse's neck and wiped sweat from his brow. He was beginning to feel calm again and was composing himself. However, every nerve and sinew was ready for a fight because he was scared of this new place and needed to be prepared.

Activity 1

Read the character description below. It is very short, but still effective; it indicates Luke's personality through his actions and emotions, and gives a reason for his actions.

Luke sat staring despondently out of the window at the grey world outside. Irritated, he shoved the glasses roughly back up his nose and tapped harshly on his thigh. He had only been grounded for a day and he was already bored with his room.

- emotions → "despondently", "Irritated"
- impatient, frustrated, angry → "tapped harshly"
- emotions reflected in the weather/setting → "grey world"

1 Write your own description of a character in three or four sentences, but don't give away all the details, just enough to get the ideas across. Include:

a) the character's emotions b) their actions c) the reason for their actions and emotions.

2 Reread your description.

a) Have you conveyed good sense of the character you were trying to create?
b) Is there any more detail about your character that you should include?

3 Consider your answers to question 2 and try to revise your character description more.

You don't need to tell the reader everything at once. It is much more effective to use small details to build a character as your writing progresses. The reader will form an impression of the character based on their actions, behaviour, thoughts, and how others react to them.

Activity 2

1 Write a second paragraph about Luke that is about what happens at the end of his grounding period. Think about the following questions:

a) How does he react?
b) Is he sorry for what he did?
c) What mood is he in?

Try to keep the paragraph concise, letting your reader fill in some of the detail.

To make your characters seem like real people to your reader, you need to think of them in this way too. They need simple details like name and age, but also physical and personal details and some relevant ideas about their life. Even if you don't tell the reader all these things, they will give the character depth in your mind and it will be evident in your writing.

Activity 3

1 Build a background for the character you created in Activity 1. Think about:

a) basic details – name, age, where they live
b) physical appearance – height, weight, hair colour
c) personality – caring, bitter, cynical, immature
d) important events in their life that may have influenced their personality (sporting success, happy childhood, broken marriage, children).

2 Highlight the details that you think would be important to include in a piece of writing. Consider whether they are important to the story or important to understanding why the character acts in the way that they do.

Knowing the background for your character will help you to keep their behaviour consistent. For instance, in the extract in Activity 1 about Luke, he is bored and frustrated at being stuck in his room. If he suddenly started playing happily it would be confusing and make the character unbelievable.

Activity 4

Read the monologue below (**Text A**). Then look at the two possible ways the woman's story could continue (**Texts B** and **C**). Both describe the arrival of a stranger who claims to be her daughter. Look carefully at the actions and reactions of the woman in each version.

Text A

I lost the photograph. An act of carelessness! I fumbled for a painkiller with aching fingers. It must have slipped from my bag then, in the supermarket, amongst the bananas. I could go back. But I realise the crates will have been changed; new bananas will have arrived from a land I can never hope to visit now.

A trip to get my shopping is my last grip on independence. They must not take that. If I am asked about the photograph I must lie, I suppose. Losing things must be a sign that I am unable to care for myself – David will likely step in and decide enough is enough – sell the house, move in with them, spend my time gratefully receiving tea and food and assistance to the bathroom. Unbearable.

Text B

It is hard to remember how I reacted when she said who she was. I know there seemed to be a long pause in time. I know I studied her face for hints, for a feeling of recognition. There were no sea reddened cheeks to help, just gently applied make up onto middle aged skin.

I stepped back to let her in then, I think. It was the eyes that so reminded me of her father's that persuaded me that this was indeed my daughter. I looked down as she passed and caught the smell of roses, it was the scent of my mother that clung to her clothes.

Text C

It was wonderful! She said she was my daughter – I knew before she spoke! I jumped a little and ran to her. I gripped her tightly, capturing the 20 years of missing her in that hug. I noticed in that hug that she smelt of my mother – roses – I felt happy that she had been looked after so well for so long! I pulled her into the house. Walking to the kitchen to make tea and collect a few biscuits; I wanted to make her feel welcome in my home.

1 **Which version is the most consistent with the woman who lost a photograph in the supermarket? Explain your answer.**

You have considered the woman's reaction to the arrival of her daughter. How would she act now?

2 **Write the next paragraph as the woman recounts how she spoke to her daughter for the first time in 20 years.**

3 **Explain the choices you have made.**

As with all monologues, the extracts in Activity 4 use the **first person narrator:** the woman is telling the story from her perspective, and uses 'I'. You could also take this approach in your narrative writing, telling the story through the eyes of one of your characters. Alternatively, you could use the **third person narrator** as shown below in an extract from *The Metamorphosis* by Franz Kafka.

Refers to character by name.

Third person – refers to character as 'he'.

As Gregor Samsa awoke one morning from uneasy dreams he found himself transformed in his bed into a gigantic insect. He was lying on his hard, as it were armor-plated, back and when he lifted his head a little he could see his domelike brown belly divided into stiff arched segments on top of which the bed quilt could hardly keep in position and was about to slide off completely. What has happened to me? he thought. It was no dream. His room, a regular human bedroom, only rather too small, lay quiet between the four familiar walls.

Recounts actions of the character.

Recounts the thoughts/ reactions of the character.

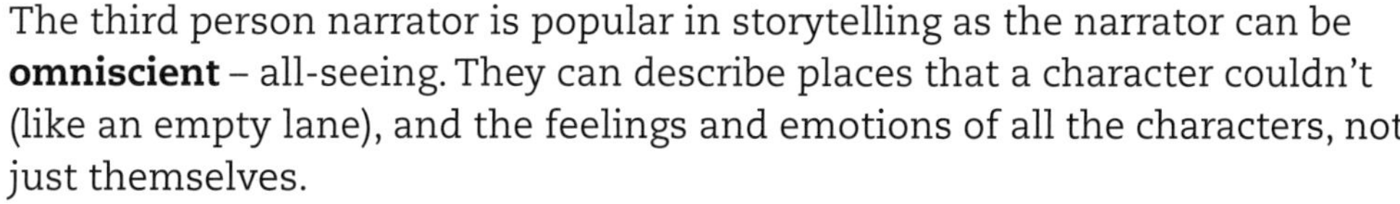

The third person narrator is popular in storytelling as the narrator can be **omniscient** – all-seeing. They can describe places that a character couldn't (like an empty lane), and the feelings and emotions of all the characters, not just themselves.

However, using the first person speaks directly to the reader, which allows them to really connect and empathise with the characters. For instance, think about your reaction to the woman who loses her photograph. It may have been sympathy, pity or sadness. If the extract was in the third person, you might have felt dispassionate and indifferent towards the woman.

Activity 5

1 **Rewrite the first paragraph of Text A about the woman losing her photograph as a third person narrative.**

2 **Imagine that the extract about Gregor Samsa was written from his perspective. Rewrite the extract as a first person narrative.**

3 **Evaluate whether either of your pieces of writing was more effective using the new narrative perspective.**

7 Writing dialogue

This lesson will help you to...

→ **write using the voice of a character**

In narrative writing, monologues and scripts you will be expected to write **dialogue**. Dialogue is a useful way of building characters and revealing their personality, thoughts and emotions. Look at the list at the bottom of page 166 for more information about how to write a successful dialogue.

Activity 1

Look at the dialogue below from *The Boy in the Striped Pyjamas* by John Boyne. It is a conversation between Bruno and his father.

commands

list

"But you will be quiet now," said Father, raising his voice and interrupting him because none of the rules of normal family life ever applied to him. "I have been very considerate of your feelings here, Bruno, because I know that this move is difficult for you. And I have listened to what you have to say, even though your youth and <u>inexperience</u> force you to phrase things in an <u>insolent manner</u>. And you'll notice that I have not reacted to any of this. But the moment has come when you will simply have to accept that – "

"I don't want to accept it!" shouted Bruno.

"Go to your room, Bruno."

1 **Explain what Boyne tells us about Father through the way that he speaks.**
   a) **What sort of personality does Father have?**
   b) **How is he feeling?**
   c) **How does he treat Bruno?**
   d) **How does Boyne use the techniques labelled and the words underlined to create this impression?**

2 **Change Father's personality and emotions by rewriting the dialogue in one of the ways given below.**

   For instance, to make Father seem uninterested, a writer could write something like: *"Yes, we are in a far off country where you don't know anyone, Bruno. Sorry, is that a problem?"*

   a) **Father is shy and sorry that he has to tell his son what to do.**
   b) **Father is unhappy and resents Bruno for making him feel bad.**
   c) **Father is an emotional person who can't decide what to do for the best.**

3 **The relationship between characters can also be revealed through dialogue. Rewrite the dialogue so that Father speaks to Bruno as if they are equals.**

4 **Look back to the character you created in Lesson 6. Write two paragraphs in which they recount events that happened to them. The stories should reveal their personality.**

ResultsPlus
Controlled assessment tip

Writing too much dialogue can make creative writing very dull to read. Your reader needs description of settings, people and reactions to help them picture what they are reading. Try to balance the amount of dialogue you use with the description you include.

Dialogue can also tell part of the story. This is called **exposition**. The character can move the story along by reporting incidents that the reader may not have known about before. In monologues the whole text is exposition as the character recounts a story and their emotions.

Here is an example of a controlled assessment task you could be expected to answer. You will be expected to structure your story effectively.

Look at this image.

Write a narrative titled 'The knock'.
(24 marks)

Activity 2

Write a response to this question:

Write two paragraphs of a narrative in response to the title 'The Knock'. Focus on how well you structure the narrative.

You should spend 20 minutes on this task.

ResultsPlus Self assessment

Before you complete this self-assessment activity, you might like to read some sample answers to this task on the following pages (132-133).

1 **Check your answer to Activity 2:**
- Have you developed your ideas throughout your writing?
- Have you organised your ideas well, using paragraphs and linking paragraphs effectively?

2 **Now try to grade your answer to Activity 2 by applying the mark scheme opposite. You will need to be careful and precise in your marking.**

■ **Band 2**
- ideas are sometimes appropriate
- some control over choice of vocabulary and sentence structure
- some appropriate use of paragraphs

● **Band 3**
- ideas are developed appropriately
- well-chosen vocabulary and some crafting of sentences
- controlled use of paragraphs and successful use of cohesive devices

▲ **Band 4**
- ideas are effective and sustained
- aptly chosen vocabulary and variety in the construction of sentences
- effective paragraphing and cohesive devices used within and between paragraphs

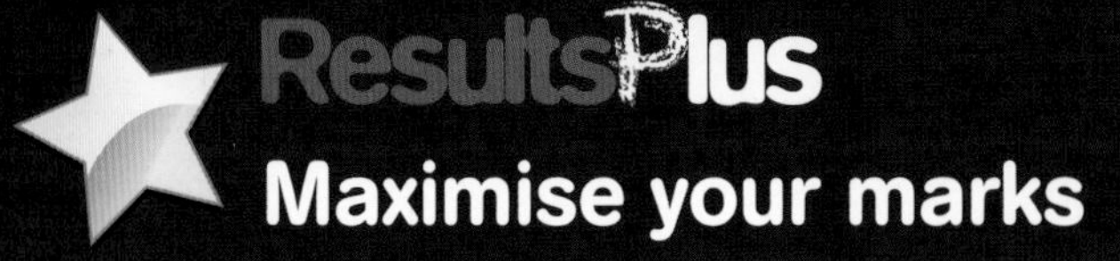

Write two paragraphs of a narrative titled 'The Knock'. You should focus on how well you structure your narrative.

Here are three student answers to the narrative task on page 131. Read the answers together with the examiner comments around and after the answers. Then complete the activity.

Student 1 – Extract typical of a grade (D) answer

Damien was rushing home because he could not wait to see his brand new motorbike. When Damien got home he was not very happy because his motorbike was not on the drive where he expected it. He went into the house, which was warm and went into the kitchen to make some cornflakes with cold milk. Then he went into the living room and sat on his leather sofa and watched his plasma screen TV. Then there was a knock at the door. Damien spilt his cereal in shock. He walked to the door very cautiously. Through the glass on the door he could see a bright yellow jacket. He opened the door to see it was his friend from work with his new motorbike.

Constant use of "then" links ideas but it is not always appropriate to organise actions in a narrative.

Good development of an idea – helping the reader to get to know Damien.

Examiner summary

This part of the answer is typical of grade D performance. Student 1 does develop the description of setting so gives the reader a good idea about the sort of character Damien is. The description of opening the door is linked with the word "then" throughout. Although this helps the reader to see that there are a series of actions, it can make the narrative dull. It is important to move between ideas so that they link more carefully.

Student 2 – Extract typical of a grade (C) answer

When Joe got home he took off his coat which was drenched with water dripping down and splashing to the floor. It was a very dark, grey rainy day so Joe switched on the lights and the fire in the living room. He slouched down on his leather sofa and turned on his new television to watch the football match. There was a knock at the door. Joe decreased the volume on the remote and stood up. There was another knock at the door. As he walked cautiously towards the door, Joe felt curious as he didn't know who it could be calling at this time. Joe was feeling nervous and opened the door carefully to see a tall policeman who didn't look friendly.

Clever use of a short sentence to make the knock on the door seem sudden – helps move the narrative on effectively.

Good use of vocabulary to develop the idea of mood and setting.

A repetition of the knock on the door is appropriate to give a sense of urgency.

Examiner summary

This part of the answer is typical of grade C performance. Student 2 has done well to develop the setting appropriately in the opening paragraph. The use of a short sentence to introduce the idea of someone at the door at the start of the second paragraph is clever and moves the narrative on well. Repeating the short sentence is effective and helps develop a sense of urgency. However, the student was unable to sustain this in the final sentence of the paragraph, as the repeated idea of "cautiously", "carefully" and "nervous" is not an appropriate development of an idea.

Student 3 – Extract typical of a grade B answer

A strong opening that gives the sense of an ending to the story.

This is a clever use of short sentences that help to build suspense in the writing.

Opening the door was a mistake. He knew that now.
Settling in front of the TV, Danny kicked off his shoes and warmed his feet by the fire. It was a dismal day outside and so was a perfect chance to settle down on his new leather sofa and watch football on the plasma.
A knock. It wasn't the time or the type of day to expect visitors. He waited a while. Should he go? His feet were warmed through and there was a chance of a goal. Another knock. Urgent. Insistent. Danny moved slowly to his door. Tugging it open he peered into the gap he created.

An effectively developed paragraph, especially the short sentences for the knock that sound sudden.

Examiner summary

This part of the answer is typical of grade B performance. Student 3 has effectively hooked the reader with the opening sentence and has given a sense the narrative has a secure structure by hinting at an event that happens later in the story. The setting and the knocking is developed appropriately and this is sustained throughout the paragraph.

ResultsPlus
Build better answers

Move from a Grade D to Grade C

In this part of your task you need to think about how you can use techniques such as repetition to develop ideas well. Student 1 should have avoided repetition of the word "then" as Student 2 did. Both students develop the idea of setting appropriately but Student 2 is able to do this more effectively when the action begins. The use of the knock on the door to begin the second paragraph is a clever structural device.

Move from a Grade C to Grade B

In this part of your task you need to stick to one strategy that you have decided from the beginning. Student 3 cleverly hooks the reader in the opening line and gives a sense of events later in the story. This allows the examiner to believe from the beginning that the narrative of the story will be secure because it is clear that the structure has been thought through. The description of the setting and the knock on the door is similar to Student 2's response. However, Student 3 remains focused on the idea they are developing.

Putting it into Practice

1. **Plan out the rest of the narrative in response to the title 'The Knock'.**
2. **Write the opening and the closing of the narrative in response to the title 'The Knock'. Remember to make connections between the opening and the closing of the narrative.**

8 Crafting vocabulary

This lesson will help you to...

→ **use language to effectively create images in the reader's mind**

As the writer, it is your job to encourage the imagination of the reader to see the people, events and worlds you create in your writing. You need to use vocabulary effectively to create images in the reader's mind.

Read this extract from *A Sound of Thunder* by Ray Bradbury. Bradbury has cleverly used vocabulary to give a sense of how powerful the dinosaur is in its actions:

It came on great **oiled**, resilient, striding legs. It <u>towered</u> thirty feet above half of the trees, a great evil god, folding its delicate watchmaker's claws close to its **oily** reptilian chest. Each lower leg was a **piston**, a thousand pounds of white bone, sunk in thick ropes of muscle, sheathed over in a gleam of **pebbled** skin like the mail of a terrible warrior. Each thigh was a ton of meat, ivory, and **steel mesh**. And from the great breathing cage of the upper body those two delicate arms dangled out front, arms with hands which might pick up and examine men like toys, while the snake neck <u>coiled</u>. And the head itself, a **ton of sculptured stone**, lifted easily upon the sky. Its mouth <u>gaped</u>, exposing a fence of teeth like **daggers**. Its eyes <u>rolled</u>, ostrich eggs, empty of all expression save hunger. It closed its mouth in a death grin. It <u>ran</u>, its pelvic bones <u>crushing</u> aside trees and bushes, its taloned feet <u>clawing</u> damp earth, leaving prints six inches deep wherever it settled its weight.

ResultsPlus
Controlled assessment tip

Using several adjectives in a row usually means that you have yet to select the right word. It is very unusual for professional writers to overuse adjectives in this way. Go through your writing and underline all the places where you have used more than one adjective - what is the one perfect word to replace this list?

Activity 1

Look at the highlighted words in the extract above.

1 **What images do the underlined verbs create in your mind?**

2 **What images do the words in bold create in your mind?**

3 **Now write your own description of a bird hatching. Select verbs to emphasise how small and vulnerable the bird is. Select vocabulary that suggests the bird is new.**

You also need to use vocabulary to create a mood or an atmosphere in your writing. In love stories you would select vocabulary that would create either a romantic or a passionate mood. In thriller writing you might select words that create anxiety or build tension.

Look at this extract from *A Ghost* by Guy de Maupassant:

I thought I heard, or rather felt, a rustle behind me. I took no notice, thinking a draught had lifted some curtain. But a minute later, another movement, almost indistinct, sent a **disagreeable** little shiver over my skin. It was so **ridiculous** to be moved like this even so slightly, that I would not turn round, being **ashamed**. I had just discovered the second package I needed, and was on the point of reaching for the third, when a great and sorrowful sigh, close to my shoulder, made me give a mad leap two yards away. In my spring I had turned round, my hand on the hilt of my sword, and surely had I not felt that, I should have fled like a coward. A tall woman, dressed in white, was facing me, standing behind the chair in which I had sat a second before.

The ghost is never mentioned explicitly but the writer cleverly increases the tension of the text so that when the woman dressed in white appears we are prepared to believe she is a ghost.

Activity 2

Look at the highlighted words in the extract.

1 **What effect do the underlined words have on the text?**

2 **What effect do the words in bold have on the text?**

3 **Write a description of a forest. Use words to describe the forest that make the reader feel increasingly uneasy.**

4 **Write a second description of the forest using softer sounding vocabulary such as 'sway' and 'dappled light' to create a calm atmosphere.**

Don't expect to always select the correct word the first time you write. Craft your writing by going back and making changes, while thinking about the effect you are trying to achieve.

ResultsPlus
Self assessment

Check your answer – have you:

- selected words that are precise and best fit the text you are writing?
- selected words that work hard and communicate more than one message?

Activity 3

Edit the following description of a beach. Experiment by changing the vocabulary to create the following moods and atmospheres:

1 **A lonely man is sitting, thinking calmly.**

2 **A murderer is somewhere on the beach and the narrator was terrified.**

The waves run up the beach and then back out to sea. Stones travel up the beach and settle, creating a line of debris on the shore. The beach curves around the cliff edge with narrow paths winding down through the rocks. The paths make the stretch of sand available to only a few.

9 Crafting sentences

This lesson will help you to...

- → **use sentence structure and punctuation to create effects.**

You can use sentences to create a particular effect on the reader. Questions can create confusion; exclamations suggest excitement or other extreme emotions. The length of sentences can also have a powerful effect in varying the pace of a piece of writing.

Look at this extract from *Twilight* by Stephanie Meyer, a book about a vampire. The writer creates tension in the writing by using lots of commas to break sentences up into a series of short phrases.

The door opened again, and the cold wind suddenly gusted through the room, rustling the papers on the desk, swirling my hair around my face. The girl who came in merely stepped to the desk, placed a note in the wire basket, and walked out again. But Edward Cullen's back stiffened, and he turned slowly to glare at me – his face was absurdly handsome – with piercing, hate-filled eyes.

Activity 1 **Use short sentences and questions to write a paragraph to describe being chased.**

Now look at the use of sentences in this extract from a love story. Here the writer has used lots of sentences, held together with commas to create a sense of Rebecca's excitement. The writer also uses lists to build this excitement.

John said he would go out with me. All thoughts of work disappeared, mind went numb, pacing around the shop, wondering what to wear, where to go, what to say. I spoke it out loud hoping it would mean I could then concentrate, "I, Rebecca Worthington, am about to date John Clarke, the gorgeous, muscle-ridden, kind, lump of a man." But no. My mind continued to whirl.

Activity 2 **Write a description of a couple meeting at a restaurant, using lists and long sentences like the author. You might also want to include occasional exclamation marks to highlight extreme emotion: for instance, 'Here he is!'**

Activity 3

1. **Practise writing a paragraph for a description titled 'and then they saw me'. Focus on the sentences you use, considering the effect they will have.**
2. **Check your choice of sentence structure and punctuation. Is it effective?**
3. **Use what you have found in your self-assessment to adjust your paragraph as necessary.**

Here is an example of a controlled assessment task you could be expected to answer. You will be expected to craft language effectively.

Look at this image.

Write a narrative titled 'The knock'. (24 marks)

Activity 4

Write a response to this question:

Write the final paragraph of a narrative titled 'The Knock'. You should focus on how well you craft the language that you use.

You should spend 10 minutes on this task.

ResultsPlus
Self assessment

Before you complete this self-assessment activity, you might like to read some sample answers to this task on the following pages (138-139).

1 **Check your answer to Activity 4:**
- Have you expressed ideas effectively?
- Have you selected vocabulary for effect?
- Have you chosen suitable punctuation and sentence structure to create an effect?

2 **Now try to grade your answer to Activity 4 by applying the mark scheme opposite. You will need to be careful and precise in your marking.**

Band 2
- ideas are expressed clearly some of the time
- vocabulary is sometimes well chosen
- some evidence of punctuation being selected for emphasis and effect
- sentences are clearly structured, with some attempt to control how they sound

Band 3
- ideas are expressed clearly
- vocabulary is well chosen
- punctuation is mostly selected for emphasis and effect
- sentences are clearly structured, with control over how they sound

Band 4
- ideas are effective throughout
- vocabulary is aptly chosen
- precise use of vocabulary for emphasis and effect
- sentences are well structured, with effective control over how they sound

Maximise your marks

Write the final paragraph for the narrative in response to the title 'The Knock'.

You should focus on how well you craft the language that you use.

Here are three student answers to the creative writing task on page 137. Read the answers together with the examiner comments around and after the answers. Then complete the activity.

Student 1 – Extract typical of a grade (D) answer

Good choice of vocabulary.

His father told him how the accident happened, it sounded horrendous. He was driving on the motorway, trying to see how fast the motorbike was, when his life flashed before his eyes. The next time he knew of he was waking up in the hospital. He found out he had a broken leg and a broken collar bone.

This commonly used phrase, known as a cliché, weakens the language used.

Examiner summary

This part of the answer is typical of grade D performance. The sentences are clearly structured and some good word choices are made. However, there is no real evidence that the choices of words, punctuation or sentences have been used for effect. The final paragraph clearly just tells the reader what happens.

Student 2 – Extract typical of a grade (C) answer

An effective short sentence to give an effect of urgency.

The police arrived. Joe and the two policemen rushed upstairs to his parent's bedroom. Nobody was there. The window was wide open and a light breeze coming through. Joe was terrified, as he knew the robber had taken his mother's jewellery and escaped without being seen. A policeman took all the notes he could and he promised they would work hard to catch the man but both Joe and the policeman knew it was likely never going to be solved.

Good choice of vocabulary – makes the room seem still.

Examiner summary

This part of the answer is typical of grade C performance. Student 2 has used an effective opening sentence to give a sense of urgency and the word choice "light breeze" helps give a sense that the room is empty. This means that some choices have been made to have an effect on the reader.

Student 3 – Extract typical of a grade (B) answer

Good verb choices used throughout.

Clever use of questions to give the effect of confusion.

A simple choice to tug open a door had changed so much. If Danny had stayed slouched on the settee, warming his feet, all would be well. Laid out on his floor was this stranger, a gash deep in his forehead. The crowd cheered. Another goal? Another victory for his team? Danny felt as if they were jeering him – mocking him – for a victorious fight that would bring his life to a close.

The dashes help build up pace in the writing and show how much the cheering is upsetting him.

Examiner summary

This part of the answer is typical of grade B performance. The punctuation and verb choices are particularly effective in this closing paragraph and these choices are made throughout the extract. The idea is effectively developed through the choice to use questions and the pattern of three to highlight his upset and confusion.

ResultsPlus
Build better answers

Move from a Grade (D) to Grade (C)

In this part of your task you need to start considering how you want the reader to react. Although written clearly, Student 1 has made no choices that are intended to have an effect on the reader. Instead, the student has written accurately about what happened. Student 2 improves on this by starting to make choices, particularly with sentences and some vocabulary, to impact on the reader.

Move from a Grade (C) to Grade (B)

In this part of your task you need to begin to vary the techniques that you use to engage and affect the reader. Student 3 has used language throughout that is intended to have an effect on the reader and the meaning in the narrative. There is much more sentence and punctuation variety than those chosen by Student 2, which makes the writing much more interesting to read.

Putting it into Practice

1 **Write the final paragraph for a narrative titled 'The Box'. Try to include a question, a short sentence for effect and verbs that have a powerful impact on the reader.**

2 **Write a second final paragraph for the same narrative. Use the same techniques but try to achieve a different effect.**

Controlled Assessment Practice

Examiner's tip

These tasks will be available for you to see from the beginning of the academic year.

Examiner's tip

Prepare before your assessment as much as you like, but all writing must be completed in the supervised controlled assessment.

Guidance for students: Creative Writing Task

What do I have to do?
You will complete one task on creative writing, from a choice of four.
You must complete this task on your own.

How much time do I have?
Following preparation, you will have up to two hours to complete this task.

How do I prepare for the task?
Choose the task.

Review the stimulus material provided for the task with your teacher. Stimulus materials will be based on themes which are shared with the Edexcel Poetry Anthology themes; **however,** it is not necessary to study the poems for the writing task. Any theme may be chosen.

You will be given guidance about creative writing, which may include:

- the content - real or imagined events
- your audience
- the 'voice' you may want to use
- any plot or narrative structure
- the structural features of your writing
- creation of character and use of dialogue
- creation of setting and atmosphere
- appropriate language techniques
- use of imagery
- use of rhetorical devices.

You should then prepare by making notes and planning your response to the task.

Examiner's tip

Practise making your writing engaging while you prepare for the exam.

Examiner's tip

Remember to check over your writing before you submit it.

What must my response to the task show?
The response must show that you can:

- write clearly, effectively, and imaginatively in your chosen form to engage the reader
- make sure your spelling, punctuation and grammatical structures are accurate and appropriate for purpose and effect.

How should students present my response?
A written response of up to 1000 words to the task.

The Creative Writing Task for the student

Choose one theme and complete the task from the choice below.

The text may be one of the following:
- Narrative
- Description
- Monologue
- Script

Examiner's tip

Answer one task below using one of these forms.

Theme A: Relationships
Task: Look at the image on the website.
Write a text which explores EITHER the events leading up to this moment OR the events which directly follow this moment.

(24)

Turn to page 142 to see the controlled assessment stimulus material

Theme B: Clashes and Collisions
Task: Look at the video clip on the website.
Write a text from the viewpoint of a person in this videoclip.

(24)

Theme C: Somewhere, Anywhere
Task: Look at the image on the website.
Write a text titled 'A place of my own'.

(24)

Theme D: Taking a Stand
Task: Listen to the podcast on the website.
Write a text based on the activities of a campaigner.

(24)

Here are the stimuli for the tasks on page 141

Relationships (image)

Robert Doisneau,
Le Baiser de l'Hotel de Ville
(1950)

Clashes and Collisions (video)

Euronews
G20 London Protests

Somehere, Anywhere (image)

'For Sale House Sign'

Taking a Stand (podcast)

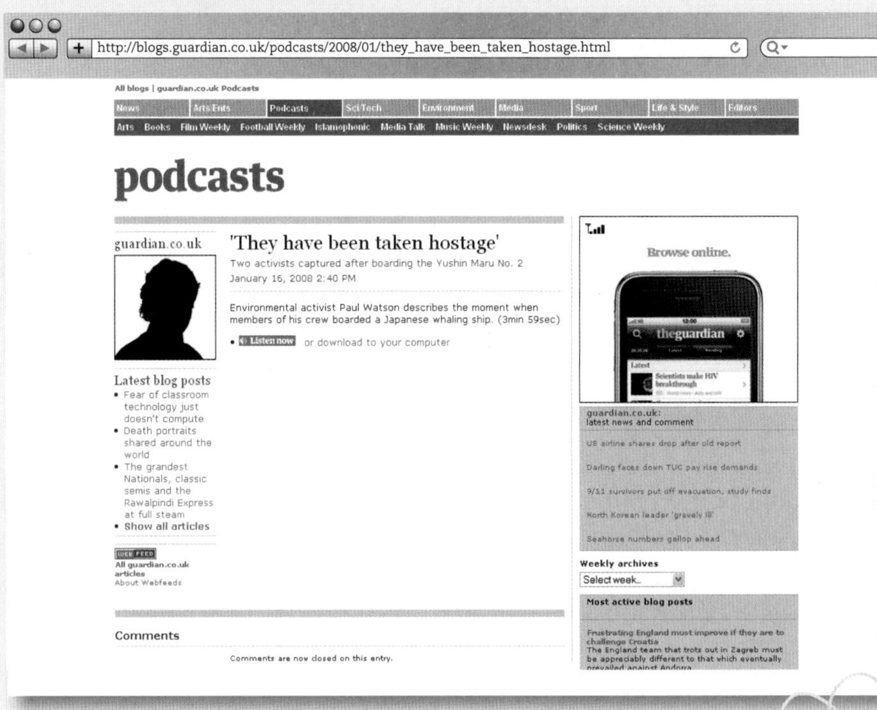

Guardian Podcast — Paul Watson (3 min 59)

Japan's whaling fleets in the Antartic halted its operations today while they decide what to do with two anti-whaling activists who've been detained by the crew of a Japanese harpoon ship that they climbed on board. This is the moment it happened…

Unit 3 Spoken Language

This unit is a GCSE English Language unit. If you are taking GCSE English, turn to Unit 3 page 114 for Creative English: Writing.

The Spoken Language unit gives you the opportunity to develop your speaking and listening skills, complete a spoken language study and produce a piece of writing for the spoken voice. This student book unit focuses on the spoken language study and spoken voice tasks.

Spoken Language is all around us. In this unit you will explore both scripted speech, for example in TV scripts and plays, and spontaneous speech, which could be your own everyday language, the language of people your age, the language you hear around you or that you hear on TV, radio and the internet.

This section of the book will help you to identify features of spoken language, both scripted and spontaneous, and to understand the effects that it has on different audiences. You will also investigate the different reasons why people choose to use language differently in certain situations. The texts and activities you will encounter as you develop these skills are all focused on helping you to achieve the best grade you can in your controlled assessment tasks.

Your assessment

This unit is a controlled assessment unit for the GCSE English Language. You will complete **two** writing tasks: a Spoken Language Study and Writing for the Spoken Voice.

In the **Spoken Language Study** section, you will complete **one** task from a choice of **two** in which you will be asked to explore the way spoken language works. You will have up to two hours to complete this task and you can write up to 1000 words. You will be given the task in advance so that you have time to plan your response so that you feel prepared to complete this part of the controlled assessment.

In your response to the spoken language task, you will need to:

- ✔ **show how spoken language changes depending on the context**
- ✔ **show understanding of some of the choices people make when they are speaking.**

In the **Writing for the Spoken Voice** section, you will complete **one** task from a choice of **three** and write either a speech, a story with lots of direct speech, or a script for a specific media type, such as a radio drama or TV soap. You will either be given a word limit of 1000 words or a limit of the equivalent of between 30 seconds and 2 minutes of spoken language. You will be given the task in advance so that you have time to plan your response so that you feel prepared to complete this part of the controlled assessment.

Your response to the writing for the spoken voice task must show that you:

- ✔ **understand that different media work in different ways**
- ✔ **understand the needs of different audiences and purposes.**

Assessment Objectives

Your response to the controlled assessment writing tasks of Unit 3 will be marked using these Assessment Objectives:

Spoken Language Study Task

- ✔ **Understand variations in spoken language, explaining why language changes in relation to contexts.**
- ✔ **Evaluate the impact of spoken language choices in your own and others' use.**

Writing for the Spoken Voice Task

- ✔ **Write to communicate clearly, effectively and imaginatively, using and adapting forms and selecting vocabulary appropriate to task and purpose in ways that engage the reader.**
- ✔ **Organise information and ideas into structures and sequenced sentences, paragraphs, and whole texts, using a variety of linguistic and structural features to support cohesion and overall coherence.**

This student book unit will help you to understand what these require you to do so that you can write a successful response to your controlled assessment writing tasks.

1 Identifying how spoken language works

This lesson will help you to...

- → understand how spoken language works
- → identify some language features and structures of spoken language

There are two main types of spoken language:

- **scripted** speech which you hear in most television programmes, films and formal speeches
- **spontaneous** speech such as conversations or answering questions in class. When written down, spontaneous speech is represented by a written transcript, which includes the words spoken, lengths of pauses, interruptions and sounds like 'umm'.

You need to understand the main differences between scripted speech and spontaneous speech.

Activity 1

Listen to today's weather forecast on the TV or radio. This is an example of scripted speech.

Then record and listen to a brief conversation between two people about yesterday's weather. This is an example of spontaneous speech.

1. **Which example was easier to understand? Why?**
2. **Which example had more pauses in the speech? Why do you think this was?**
3. **Did you spot any repetition in either example? Why do you think this was?**
4. **Did the two people having the conversation interrupt each other or speak at the same time? Why do you think this happened?**

ResultsPlus
Controlled assessment tip

Don't treat spontaneous spoken language as an inferior form of written language. Think about the way you and the people around you speak. What forms do they use, and what sounds appropriate?

Here are some of the features of spontaneous speech:

- **Pauses** – silences, indicating thinking time, uncertainty or a change in subject. In transcripts these are indicated in brackets either with the length of pause in seconds (3) or as a brief pause (.)
- **Interruptions/Overlaps** – when one speaker is interrupted by another. Sometimes people interrupt because they are excited about what is being said; sometimes they are just rude and don't wait for their turn! Sometimes speech overlaps because one speaker thought the other had finished. In transcripts this is indicated by //
- **Incomplete utterances** – when a speaker begins to speak but does not complete the thought. Sometimes people change their mind about what they want to say; sometimes there is no need to complete the thought because the meaning is obvious.
- **Hedges** – ways of making a statement less certain: for example, 'I believe that', 'it seems that', 'perhaps'. People sometimes think it is rude to make definite statements, particularly if they are correcting someone.
- **Fillers** – words used to fill in pauses while the speaker is thinking: for example, 'you know'.
- **Non-verbal sounds** – sounds used to fill a pause or to encourage another speaker to continue: for example, 'hmm', 'erm'.
- **Ellipsis** – where words are left out, often because the meaning is clear: for example, 'I caught the bus but Julie didn't' [catch the bus]
- **Repetition** – people often repeat words or ideas, especially if they are excited.

Activity 2

Compare these two examples of spoken language:

Example A

Mavis: You've got to have something before you go out.
Derek: I haven't time, have I. Why, Mavis? Why did we have to oversleep today of all days? I just hope this isn't going to be an omen.
Mavis: An omen?
Derek: Yes, Mavis. An omen. I've got three important meetings today. Prospective new clients. And if the day finishes the way it's started…well, it doesn't bear thinking about.

Example B

Cathy: Carly's been smacking //me
Sam: // This way //
Cathy: Alright (exclamation) (sees food)
Sam: I'll sit next to you
Cathy: Erm (.) by the way
Sam: Mm
Cathy: Erm (.) do you like strawberries
Sam: Yes a lot (.) that's my favourite food
Cathy: Do you like ice cream
Sam: Yes
Cathy: Good (.) 'cos we've got we've got that for supper

1 Which one is spontaneous speech and which one is scripted speech? How do you know?

2 Find one example of each of the following features of spontaneous speech in the relevant example:

a) pause b) filler c) incomplete utterance d) repetition

ResultsPlus
Controlled assessment tip

Make sure you give examples when you are explaining how spoken language works. For example: The use of a pause in the sentence 'I don't think (1) no it's not' indicates that the speaker might be confused or unsure.

2 Identifying the features of spoken language

This lesson will help you to...

→ identify more language features and structures of spoken language

Recognising the features of spoken language can tell you how a speaker is feeling or what their attitude is towards either another speaker or the topic.

Activity 1

Read this transcript :

A: I'm just teaching my (.) two of my daughters to drive(.) one's already got a provisional licence cos she's seventeen(.) the other's sixteen so she can't get a provisional licence until her birthday(.) so (.) with her the youngest Sarah (.) we have to go to the big car park at the supermarket (.) we just drive around there (.) but it's quite useful I mean (.)she can get to know the basics //there //

B: Is it actually legal (.) on a car park

A: Well er yeah (.) it is because you're you're not actually (.) er you know (.) on (.) the public highway (.) and therefore // (.) //

B: //mm//

A: it may be that you shouldn't be on their premises (.) er but (.) you certainly don't need to have a licence to drive on// (.) // you know (.) // places // like that you

1 **How does Speaker A (the father) respond when asked if it's legal for his daughter to drive in the car park?**

2 **Find two examples of spoken language features which show his feelings or attitude.**

ResultsPlus
Controlled assessment tip

Don't assume that a feature of spontaneous spoken language is always there for the same reason. Look at the *context*. For example, a speaker might pause to think what to say, but he or she might also pause to show that they disagree, or that they don't approve of something another speaker has said.

When you write you are expected to use complete sentences, following the rules you have been taught. This is not true of spontaneous speech as you don't have much time to think before you speak. People often use non-standard language forms – vocabulary and grammar that do not follow the rules of written Standard English.

For example:

- non-standard vocabulary – 'Hey' to mean 'Hello'
- non-standard grammar – 'Wow, did I mess up today!'

Activity 2

Read the transcript of a conversation below:

A: Hey //could//you do me a quick favour
B: //mm// yup yup
A Grab that bit of paper by you and chuck it over here
B: Sure okay hang on a tick and I'll just get it for //you//
A //cheers//

1 **Find two examples of non-standard language. What would be the Standard English equivalent of these terms?**

2 **Does one of the speakers have speech patterns closer to Standard English, or do the two speakers use standard and non-standard language in a similar way? Discuss possible reasons for the language choices.**

3 **Rewrite the transcript as a script, in full sentences.**

ResultsPlus
Controlled assessment tip

When you identify a feature of spontaneous spoken language, explain *why* it is there. For example, 'She pauses and then uses a non-verbal response because she doesn't agree with what her friend is saying: '(2) mm.'

Spoken language is often not precise. People use vague terms, especially if the conversation is exploring unfamiliar ideas or a challenging topic. For example:

- To describe an unfamiliar object you might say, 'It's sort of this big with a handle-type thing on top and knob thingies on the side.'
- When discussing a sensitive topic you might say, 'I kind of think this type of thing is personal and there is no right answer really, but for me...'

Activity 3

Choose one of these objects:

kettle	pencil sharpener	laptop	mobile phone
corkscrew	smoothie	Maths text book	sewing machine

1 **Describe the object to someone without using its name and without using gestures. If possible, record your speech or ask another student to write down what you say.**

2 **What do you notice about the words you used to describe the object?**

3 Understanding contexts 1

This lesson will help you to...

- → understand how different contexts affect spoken language choices
- → explore the way language changes according to where the speakers live and their background
- → explore how language affects attitudes towards people and situations

The way people choose to speak is influenced by different contexts such as:

- **place** – where they live and where they were born/brought up.
- **time** – language changes with time. New words and phrases come into a language constantly, slang changes very rapidly, and social rules of language - for example, rules of formality - may also change.
- **gender** – gender and whether they are speaking to males, females or both.
- **age** – their age and the age of the person/people they are speaking to.
- **audience** – the relationship between the speakers, the roles they are taking and their relative status.
- **situation/purpose** – where and why the speech is taking place.

Activity 1

This activity will help you to think about how your choice of language is affected by your **audience** – their age, their gender and your relationship with them.

1 Think about and note down how you might greet each of these people:

a) your mother/father b) a baby c) your teacher
d) an interviewer e) a boyfriend/girlfriend

2 Compare your responses with a classmate's. Would you make similar language choices?

3 Discuss other factors that might affect your language choices when greeting the people listed above: for example, how you were feeling, whether you parted on good terms.

4 How would your parents greet the people listed above? Are there any differences?

5 How do you think your grandparents would greet them?

6 Discuss whether you think gender changes the way people greet each other.

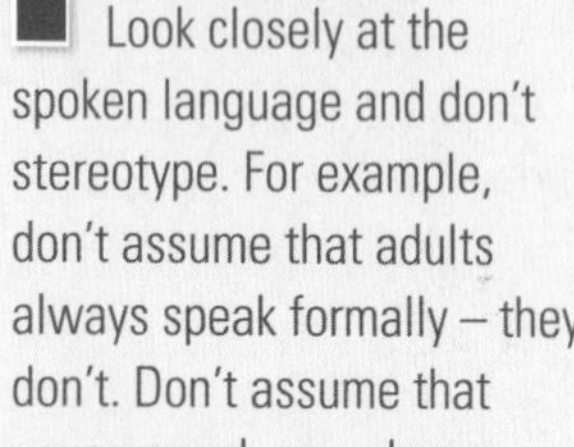

Look closely at the spoken language and don't stereotype. For example, don't assume that adults always speak formally – they don't. Don't assume that young people are always casual – they aren't.

Speech is affected by where you were born as well as where you are now – this is the context of place. Place affects the words people use and the way they sound:

- **Dialect** is the use of non-standard grammatical forms and vocabulary that is specific to a region. For instance, 'ah bist' to mean 'how are you?' (used in the Black Country), 'youse' to mean 'you' (Liverpool), 'nesh' to mean 'tender or soft' (the Potteries – Staffordshire). **Standard English (SE)** is the grammar and vocabulary of language generally accepted as 'correct'.
- **Accent** is the way words are pronounced: for instance, you might speak with a Birmingham accent, a Cockney (London) accent, a Geordie (Newcastle) accent. **Received Pronunciation (RP)** is a social accent. It is not associated with any specific region, and is widely used when teaching English to speakers of other languages. Very few English speakers use RP.

ResultsPlus
Watch out!

Standard English is a dialect and can be spoken with a regional accent. Don't confuse Received Pronunciation with Standard English.

Activity 2

Read the transcript of a woman from South Yorkshire speaking and answer the following questions.

Ye see wi' us thi' wo' none'r this beein' nasty t'people 'cos thi an't got right Stuff (1.0) We wo' brought up not t'ever stare at anyone and not to tek p__ aht on people who didn't 'ave right clothes because none'r us 'ad owt (.) But it in't like that now (1.0) Ah never wanted owt (.) an' 'ave been 'appy wi mi life 'cos Ah knew Ah couldn't ever 'ave owt else

Omission of letters from a swear word

1. List the vocabulary in this transcript that is not found in Standard English.
2. List the grammatical forms that are not found in Standard English.
3. Explain what the effect would be if the speaker had used Standard English.

Cultural background also influences the way people speak. People from close-knit ethnic or religious groups may have vocabulary or expressions known only to that group, for example.

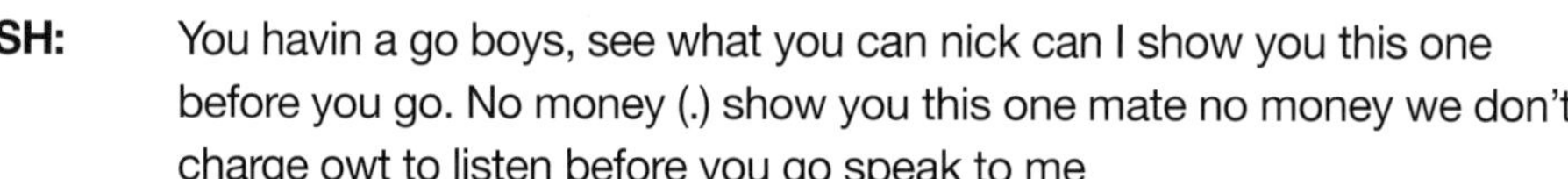

Activity 3

Listen to the conversation between a fairground stallholder and three boys. The transcript is below.

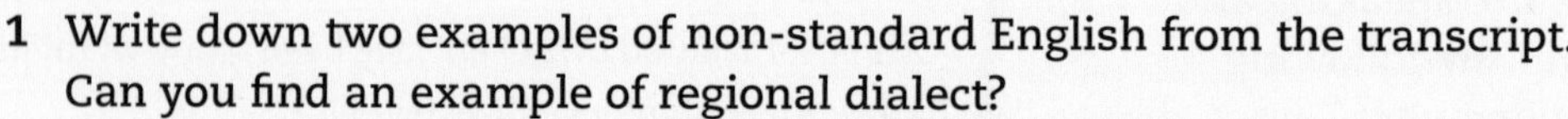

SH: You havin a go boys, see what you can nick can I show you this one before you go. No money (.) show you this one mate no money we don't charge owt to listen before you go speak to me

Boy A: I might as well, how much is it

SH: It's a dead easy game mate it's 50 pence mate you get 3 shots all you've got to do mate is knock over the golf tee to win (.) get a prize if you lose mate (3.0) that's it are you havin a go

Boy A: Yeah

1. **Write down two examples of non-standard English from the transcript. Can you find an example of regional dialect?**
2. **Write down an example of Standard English.**
3. **What differences can you identify between the spoken English of the stallholder and the spoken English of Boy A?**

ResultsPlus
Controlled assessment tip

Remember that everyone has a range of styles when they are talking. No one is always formal, no one is always casual. Remember the *context*.

Sharing accent and dialect makes people feel part of the group and gives them a sense of belonging. However, some people might associate the use of accent and dialect with lower social status. People sometimes change their language to avoid this, depending on the context. For example:

- We often use Standard English and formal language in a job interview.
- Some people have a special 'telephone voice' using Standard English and Received Pronunciation.

There are other ways in which language can influence the way people think about each other:

- We use language to encourage people to like or admire us. For instance, we use terms of endearment, such as 'dear', when addressing people who are close to us. Or we might address someone as 'Sir' or 'Mr'/'Mrs' to show respect.
- We select language that persuades people to share our perspective. We might choose very positive language: for example, 'amazing', 'superb', 'best ever', or language to gain sympathy: for example, 'cute', 'tragic'.
- Sometimes we use derogatory language that hurts others.

Activity 4

1 Can you think of any times you have changed the way you speak to fit the context? (Think about social and more formal contexts you have been in.)

ResultsPlus
Build better answers

Look at this part of a controlled assessment task:

Using two examples of spoken language, comment on the way teenagers adapt their spoken language to suit the situation.

Comment on how the purpose of the spoken language affects the way it is used.

■ A Band 2 answer includes **awareness/understanding** of the ways spoken language changes according to the relevant contexts. For example: *Teenagers use a lot of informal language when they are talking to their friends...*

● A Band 3 answer shows **clear understanding** of the ways in which spoken language changes according to context and why these changes occur. For example: *Like most people, teenagers change their language depending on who they are talking to and why. They will speak casually to their parents, but they won't use the same language they use when they are with their friends.*

▲ A Band 4 answer shows **assured understanding** of the ways spoken language changes according to context and why these changes occur by explaining the different ways teenagers might adapt their language. For example: *Teenagers adapt their language depending on the group they are with and the situation they are in. Their language will be very different when they are with their friends, when they are with other teenagers they don't know well, when they are talking to their teachers or other adults.*

4 Understanding contexts 2

This lesson will help you to...

→ understand some of the ways in which age, gender and time affect language choices and behaviour

The **age** of the people you speak to can influence your language choices and your behaviour. For instance, when people are speaking to children they tend to use simpler sentence constructions and a limited range of vocabulary. They might also try to correct the child's language, as in the following conversation.

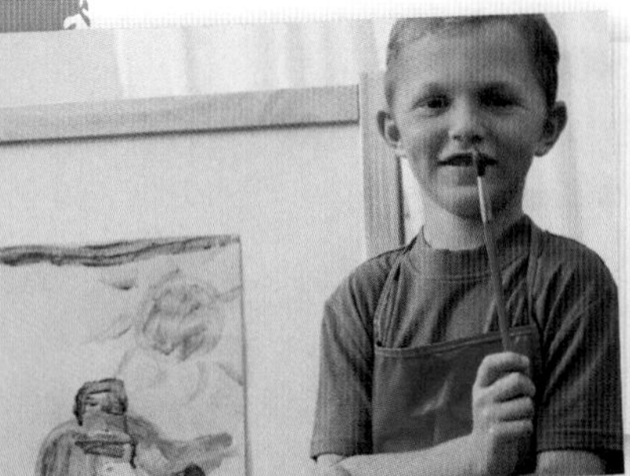

Adult: What did you do at school today?

Child: I **drawed** a picture.

Adult: Oh, you *drew* a picture?

Child: Yes, I **drawed** a picture of a car!

Teenagers often use non-standard vocabulary or **slang** terms when communicating with each other.

Activity 1

Say wHat?

Make a list of at least five slang terms that you use that your parents would not understand.

1 Where would you use these terms?
2 When would you use these terms?
3 When would you *not* use these terms? Why not?

Gender is another context that influences our language choice and behaviour. Typically, males tend to dominate the conversation and females encourage them to do so. It is often stated that males often introduce new topics; women are more concerned with politeness and supporting the other participants in the conversation.

Activity 2

Record a conversation between two males and two females. Listen carefully to the conversation, making notes on these questions:

1 Do the males or females speak the most?
2 Do the females encourage the males to speak?
3 Do the females support each other?
4 Who is responsible for introducing new topics into the conversation?
5 Are the females more polite than the males?

Taking turns in conversations is very important. If you speak for too long you will lose the attention and respect of the rest of the group. People who do this are often regarded as rude or boring.

Here are some ways that people know when it is their turn to speak:

- The speaker shows that they have finished by lowering their voice.
- The speaker looks at someone else for their support or to get their opinion.
- The speaker asks a question that requires a response, or says something like 'innit' to get confirmation of what has been said.

ResultsPlus
Controlled assessment tip

Spoken language is often economical. People tend to say only as much as they need to communicate with the people they are speaking to.

Activity 3

1 Give two examples of how the people in the conversation in Activity 2 indicate when they have finished speaking.

Spoken language also alters over **time**. For instance:

- Slang changes: a recording from the war years might refer to England as 'Blighty'.
- Some words change in meaning: 'naughty' used to mean 'wicked', but now it means 'disobedient'.
- Some words disappear from the language completely: for example, 'peradventure' meaning 'possibly'.

Activity 4

1 Watch a video clip of a documentary from before 1950, such as those available on the BFI screenonline.org.uk website.

2 Note down any unfamiliar vocabulary used and find out its meaning.

5 Understanding language choices

This lesson will help you to...

- → understand the concepts of register and tone
- → understand the different levels of formality used for different audiences and purposes

You have seen in the last two lessons that people can adapt their language to suit the context you are speaking in. Language also changes to suit their audience and your purpose through varying the register and tone.

- **Register** means the level of formality you use in particular situations and for particular audiences. Some occasions and audiences are formal and require use of Standard English; others are more relaxed and require less formal language.
- **Tone** reflects the audience and purpose for which you are speaking. You might use a serious tone for a political discussion or an older audience. A conversation between younger people might have a more humorous tone.

Activity 1

Read the conversation below between a police officer and a victim.

1 Write a sentence about each of the underlined sections, commenting on:

a) the tone of what is said

b) what the tone reveals about the speaker's attitudes and feelings

c) the level of formality used, and how this is appropriate for the audience

The text annotations are provided to help you get started.

Formal opening from the person in charge of the interview, but an obvious attempt to be friendly.

The officer has changed the topic from greetings to a request for details of the matter he has come to discuss. The victim is gathering her thoughts and clarifies what the officer has said. He mentions 'an incident' and she defines this more clearly.

'Hiya' is informal and suggests that the victim wants to be friendly in return. She also makes a standard reply to the question about health. This is quite formal, but relaxed.

Officer: Hello there, how are you?

Victim: Oh hiya, I'm fine thank you, are you?

Officer: Yes fine thanks, now then, my name's PC D____ and I understand you've got an incident to report.

Victim: Oh, erm, yeah, that's right, I'm the lady who was burgled.

Officer: Ah yes, I remember, <u>well if you'd like to come into this room</u> we could perhaps discuss the event somewhere a little quieter.

Victim: Oh yeah, that's fine.

Officer: Right then, are you able to tell me what happened?

Victim: <u>Erm...well, I was lying in bed and erm...I sensed...I thought</u> I heard Ben barking, he's my dog. He was barking quite loudly.

Officer: And when was this?

Victim: It was...it happened yesterday, last night in fact, I was lying in bed, <u>erm, I think...I think it was probably about 11:00pm.</u>

Officer: – <u>Okay...</u>

Victim: <u>//It's hard to//</u>

Officer: <u>//And what did//</u> you think when your dog was barking?

Spoken language can have many different purposes: to teach, to gather information, to entertain and so on. Conversations with a practical purpose rather than a social one are often brief and quite formal.

Activity 2

Read the conversation between Speaker A, who is asking for directions to York, and Speaker B, who is giving the directions. Look carefully at A's contribution to the conversation.

A: Erm (.) I seem to be (.) a bit lost. I'm trying to get to York.
B: Oh (.) oh well that's quite straightforward from here (.) if you just carry on down this road this is Heslington Lane // (.) // just
A: // Yeah //
B: carry on straight ahead // (.) the // road
A: // Yeah //
B: forks to the left but (.) ignore that just go straight ahead (.) and that's Broadway (0.5) when you come to the end of Broadway there are a set of traffic lights
A: Yes how far's that?
B: Oh (0.5) mile (.) probably
A: Go straight ahead for a mile
B: Yes
A: Ignore the left // fork //
B: // Ignore // the left fork
A: Yeah (.) then I get to some traffic lights
B: You get to some traffic lights (.) turn right at the traffic lights // (.) // carry
A: // huhuh //

1 **What is the tone of the conversation? Is it serious? Humorous? Light-hearted? Give two language examples that support your answer.**
2 **Find one example of a non-standard form used by Speaker A that suggests informality.**
3 **Find one example of a standard form used by Speaker A that suggests a more formal register.**

Sometimes the purpose of spoken language is social – to keep in touch with people and build relationships with them. When we do this, we use a lot of informal expressions to express or reinforce our relationship with the other person, such as 'Hi. How are you?' We might also use language that allows us to connect with the other person, like slang or dialect.

ResultsPlus
Controlled assessment tip

Try to develop the points you make about spoken language. Remember that there are different kinds of casual language, different kinds of formal language, and a lot of variety in between.

ResultsPlus
Build better answers

Look at this part of a controlled assessment task: **Using two examples of spoken language, comment on the way teenagers adapt their spoken language to suit the situation.** Comment on how language use influences other speakers and listeners.

■ A Band 2 answer includes **some awareness** of the ways in which language use may influence other speakers and listeners.

● A Band 3 answer shows **clear understanding** of the ways in which language use may influence other speakers and listeners and why this occurs.

▲ A Band 4 answer shows **thorough understanding** of the language choices speakers may make, the influence these may have on other speakers and listeners and why this occurs.

Activity 3

Perform the following role-plays with a partner. If possible record the conversations.

A: A conversation between a parent and a teenager after the teenager has been suspended from school for refusing to wear the school tie correctly.

B: Two teenagers on their way to a lunchtime detention because they were reported for not having their shirts tucked in.

1. Is the conversation formal or informal? What language shows the level of formality?
2. How does the relationship between the speakers affect the level of formality?
3. Is slang used? Is this affected by the age of the participants in the conversation?
4. Did one person speak more than the other in the conversations? What does this tell you about who is dominant in the conversation? Is this what you would have expected?
5. What is the role of the parent in conversation A? Does this affect the type of language they use?
6. Do one person's language choices affect the way another person responds?

Activity 4

Look at this example of informal conversation. Try to read it out loud.

K: I dun't know why people 'ave kids (.) me
X: Oh Karl (.) How can you say that (.) Tha can't beat 'em (0.5) Tha can't beat 'avin' a little girl come an' sit in yer lap an' put 'er arms around yer an' se'(.) Ah love you daddy (.) an' sayin' (.) I love you too dear (1.0) This mornin'(.) ah've got up an 'ad t 'ave sugar frosties wi ' y 'er and then ah 'ad to watch Grange Hill wi' y 'er (1.0) Tha cant beat it (1.5)

1. Write down the words or expressions in this conversation that create a warm, friendly tone.
2. How well do you think the two men know each other? What language clues tell you this?
3. Rewrite the conversation, changing the dialect terms to Standard English. How does this change the register and tone?

Here is an example of a controlled assessment task you could be expected to answer.

You will be expected to comment on how the purpose of the spoken language affects the way it is used.

Using two examples of spoken language, comment on the way teenagers adapt their spoken language to suit the situation.

You should comment on:
- how the purpose of the spoken language affects the way it is used
- how language use influences other speakers and listeners
- the level of formality
- the use of slang
- who speaks most if there is more than one speaker.

(24 marks)

Activity 5

Write a response to the following question:

Using two different examples of teenagers' spoken language when they are talking with their friends outside school and talking with their teachers in class, comment on some of the ways the purpose of the spoken language affects the way they speak.

You should spend 20 minutes on this question.

ResultsPlus Self assessment

Before you complete this self-assessment activity, you might like to read some sample answers to this task on the following pages (160-161).

1 **Check your answer to Activity 5:**
- Did you give examples of spoken language features?
- Did you explain how these features relate to the purpose of the spoken language?
- Have you developed this explanation clearly?

2 **Now try to grade your answer to Activity 5 by applying the mark scheme below. You will need to be careful and precise in your marking.**

Band 2
- explains how spoken language works
- includes general examples
- includes some detail about the effect one person's language may have on another person.

Band 3
- clearly explains how spoken language works
- explains how and why spoken language may change depending on the situation
- includes some examples
- shows understanding of how other people may respond to another person's spoken language, and why.

Band 4
- explains in detail how spoken language works
- explains in detail how and why spoken language changes depending on the situation
- includes good examples to support what you have said
- explains in detail how and why other people may respond to other people's spoken language, and why.

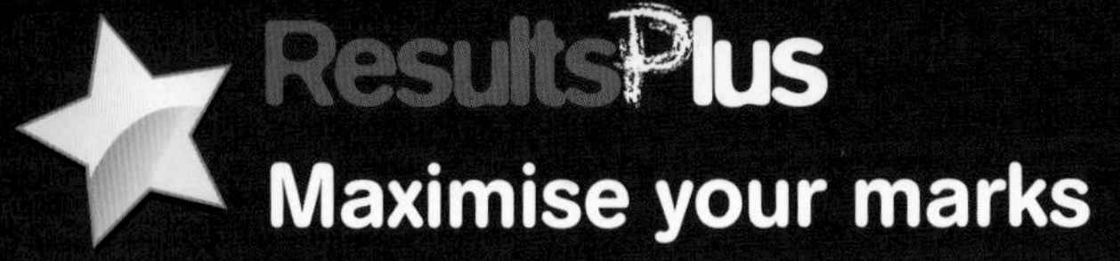

Using two examples of spoken language, comment on the way teenagers adapt their spoken language to suit the situation.

Here are three student answers to the writing about spoken language task on page 159. Read the answers, together with the examiner comments around and after the answers. Then complete the activity.

Student 1 – Extract typical of a grade (D) answer

A good general point, but needs supporting with some examples.

When the three girls are talking to each other, they use a lot of casual language. They interrupt each other a lot and no one really talks more than anyone else. When they are talking to their teachers, they are more polite. The teacher says most and no one interrupts her.

A good point, but it would be useful to know why.

Examiner summary

This part of the answer is typical of grade D performance. The student shows a clear awareness that teenagers adapt their language when they are in different situations, and gives some examples of how they might do this. Some more specific examples, to explain how the teenagers' language is more polite when they are talking to the teacher, would improve the answer.

Student 2 – Extract typical of a grade (C) answer

Good use of examples to make the explanation clear.

When me, Carl and Amy are talking, we are just chatting. There is no real purpose to what we are saying, we are just having a normal conversation. We use slang like 'crap,' 'bruv' and 'hater.' We don't interrupt each other, but Carl usually talks the most. In class, when the teacher is talking to us, we don't interrupt. If I am having a conversation with the teacher, we might be quite friendly, but I don't use slang when I am talking to her, and I don't swear. No one in our class would do that.

A good point that shows awareness of the ways a teenager adapts his or her language.

Examiner summary

This part of the answer is typical of grade C performance. The use of a very specific situation allows the student to comment on specific features and discuss the reasons why these are used. The student is aware that conversations between friends don't have an easily defined purpose, and understands that teenagers, like everyone else, vary their language depending on the situation.

Student 3 – Extract typical of a grade B answer

Teenagers will probably be more casual when they are talking with their peers, using slang, maybe swearing, but even then, their language will vary from situation to situation. My first example is a group of close friends talking. They know each other very well, the turn taking is very smooth with no interruptions and very little overlap. They use a lot of ellipsis and incomplete forms, for example when Stu says 'It was (.) you know,' and Ben and Adam say 'Yeah' because they understand what he is saying. He doesn't need to say any more. When Stu is discussing his work with his teacher, there is much less of this ellipsis. She says a lot more than he does. Stu listens and uses non-verbal sounds like 'mm' or makes short responses like 'yeah.'

Shows a thorough understanding of the ways in which spoken language works.

A good point supported by a very good example.

Examiner summary

This part of the answer is typical of grade B performance. This answer shows a thorough understanding of the way spoken language works. The student shows that they know spoken language will vary in a range of ways and they don't make the simplistic point that teenagers will speak casually when talking to their peers and formally to teachers. The student makes the very good point that close friends often don't need to say a lot to understand each other (they can use what is called 'implicit language').

ResultsPlus

Build better answers

Move from a Grade D to Grade C

In this part of the task you need to show you understand how spoken language works. In the example, the student could have identified a specific spoken language feature, such as ellipsis or slang, and explained why the speaker has used this feature. The ideas about casual language, situation and politeness could have been developed with some explanation, and some examples.

Move from a Grade C to Grade B

In this part of your task you need to show that you understand in detail how spoken language works. The student shows a clear understanding of the examples given. The main difference between Student 2 and Student 3 is that Student 3 has developed the discussion from the specific examples they are using to make more general points about the ways teenagers adapt their language.

Putting it into Practice

1 **Discuss with a partner other situations in which teenagers might alter their language, how they might do this and why.**

2 **Is teenagers' language different from adult language? Discuss this with your partner.**

6 Writing a script

This lesson will help you to...

→ understand the basic conventions of writing different types of script

In your Writing for the Spoken Voice controlled assessment task you will be given a choice of writing a script, a speech or a story with a focus on dialogue.

Writing a script is a very different process from taking part in spontaneous speech. A script is planned and written in advance to achieve a particular effect.

A script can be used for many different media types including: **staged plays, radio plays, films, TV drama, sitcoms, monologues** and **graphic novels**.

Here are the common features or **conventions** found in scripts for plays:

- **setting the scene** – description of stage set, date/time, lighting and sound, and sometimes details about the characters
- **stage directions** – movement of characters about the stage, facial expression and gestures, exits and entrances
- **layout** – divisions into acts and scenes, the name of the speaker in the margin, a new line when the speaker changes

An example of each convention is highlighted in the following extract from *Hobson's Choice* by Harold Brighouse.

Setting the scene

The SCENE represents the interior of Hobson's Boot Shop in Chapel Street, Salford.
The shop windows and entrance from the street occupy the left side. Facing the audience is the counter, with exhibits of boots and slippers, behind which the wall is filled with racks containing boot boxes. Cane chairs in front of the counter. There is a desk down L with a chair. A door R leads up to the house. In the centre of the stage is a trap leading to the cellar where work is done. There are no elaborate fittings. There are gas brackets in the windows and walls...

Sitting behind the counter are Hobson's two younger daughters, ALICE who is twenty-three, and VICTORIA, who is twenty-one, and very pretty. ALICE is knitting and VICTORIA is reading. They are in black, with neat black aprons. The door opens, and MAGGIE enters. She is Hobson's eldest daughter, thirty.

ALICE. Oh, it's you. I hoped it was father going out.
MAGGIE. It isn't. *(She crosses and takes her place at the desk).* — Stage directions
ALICE. He is late this morning.
Layout Speaker name
MAGGIE. He got up late. *(She busies herself with an account book).*
VICKEY. *(reading)* Has he had breakfast yet, Maggie?
MAGGIE. Breakfast! With a Masons' meeting last night?
VICKEY. He'll need reviving.
ALICE. Then I wish he'd go and do it.
VICKEY. Are you expecting anyone, Alice?
ALICE. Yes, I am, and you know I am, and I'll thank you both to go when he comes.
VICKEY. Well, I'll oblige you, Alice, if father's gone out first, only you know I can't leave the counter till he goes.

(ALBERT PROSSER enters from the street. He is twenty-six, nicely dressed, as the son of an established solicitor would be. He crosses to the counter and raises his hat to Alice)

ResultsPlus
Controlled assessment tip

Don't include the features of spontaneous spoken language in your script. For example, pauses, filled pauses, non-verbal sounds or similar features.

Activity 1

1 Script the next 10 lines of the play above. Make sure you:
a) use the correct layout
b) include at least one stage direction
c) try to copy the formal style of speech used by the family.

Activity 2

Now study this script from *Translations* by Brian Friel:

Act 1

Jimmy: Isn't that what I'm always telling you? Black soil for corn? That's what you should have put in that upper field of yours – corn, not spuds.

Doalty: Would you listen to that fella! Too lazy by Jasus to wash himself and he's lecturing me on agriculture! Would you take a running race at yourself, Jimmy Jack Cassie! *(Grabs Sarah)* Come away out of this with me, Sarah, and we'll plant some corn together.

Manus: Alright – alright. Let's settle down and get some work done. I know Sean Beag isn't coming – he's at the salmon. What about the Donnelly twins? *(To Doalty)* Are the Donnelly twins not coming any more?
(Doalty shrugs and turns away.) Did you ask them?

Doalty: Haven't seen them. Not about these days.
(Doalty begins whistling through his teeth. Suddenly the atmosphere is silent and alert.)

Doalty: No.

Manus: Where are they then?

Doalty: How would I know?

Bridget: Our Seamus says two of the soldiers' horses were found last night at the foot of the cliffs at Machaire Buide and… *(She stops suddenly and begins writing with chalk on her slate.)*

Non-standard language to recreate typical Irish accent and dialect

1 **Find three examples of the conventions of script layout.**
2 **What does the stage direction in line 8 tell you about Doalty's attitude?**
3 **Friel has used Irish dialect to make his characters sound realistic. Write down two more examples of non-standard forms from the script.**

Because scripted writing is planned, words can be chosen to achieve a certain effect, such as to create an atmosphere, or to show relationships between characters.

Activity 3

1 **Write a short playscript (no more than 10 lines) set in your form room just before registration. Two people are discussing a television programme. Make sure you:**
   a) **begin by setting the scene**
   b) **use the correct layout**
   c) **include at least two stage directions**
   d) **use realistic dialogue for your characters.**

7 Writing a speech or narrative

This lesson will help you to...

→ understand the basic conventions of writing speeches and narratives

ResultsPlus
Controlled assessment tip

A speech is always targeted at a specific audience, which can be narrow or broad. A script for a speech needs to show audience awareness. One way to do this is to use direct audience address. Do you want to use 'you' (exclusive) or 'we' (inclusive), or a mix of both of these?

Speeches also have conventions. They often include:

- **rhetorical questions** – a question that does not require an answer: for example, 'Do we really want that to happen?'
- **figurative language** – simile, metaphor, personification. For example, 'We are embarking upon a voyage of discovery.'
- **triads** – a list of three things to reinforce an important point. For example, 'We see this in our neighbourhoods, our schools, our homes.'
- **repetition** – repeating ideas one or more times to emphasise the point
- **facts and figures** – data, percentages, dates to support ideas
- **celebrity endorsement** – quoting famous people in support of an idea. For example, 'As teenagers we have to cope with peer pressure in many aspects of our lives, which can be very difficult, for as J.K. Rowling wrote "It takes a great deal of courage to stand up to your enemies, but even more to stand up to your friends."'
- **personal pronouns** – using 'I' or 'We' to suggest that the audience shares the speaker's ideas.

Activity 1

Read the extract below from President Obama's inaugural speech.

My fellow citizens:

I stand here today humbled by the task before us, grateful for the trust you have bestowed, mindful of the sacrifices borne by our ancestors. I thank President Bush for his service to our nation, as well as the generosity and cooperation he has shown throughout this transition.

Forty-four Americans have now taken the presidential oath. The words have been spoken during rising tides of prosperity and the still waters of peace. Yet, every so often the oath is taken amidst gathering clouds and raging storms. At these moments, America has carried on not simply because of the skill or vision of those in high office, but because We the People have remained faithful to the ideals of our forbearers, and true to our founding documents.

So it has been. So it must be with this generation of Americans.

That we are in the midst of crisis is now well understood. Our nation is at war, against a far-reaching network of violence and hatred. Our economy is badly weakened, a consequence of greed and irresponsibility on the part of some, but also our collective failure to make hard choices and prepare the nation for a new age. Homes have been lost; jobs shed; businesses shuttered. Our health care is too costly; our schools fail too many; and each day brings further evidence that the ways we use energy strengthen our adversaries and threaten our planet.

1 For each of the following examples of the conventions of speeches, write a sentence stating how it helps Obama to get his message across:
   a) triad: 'Homes have been lost; jobs shed; businesses shuttered.'
   b) metaphor: 'gathering clouds and raging storms'
   c) personal pronoun: 'We the People...'

2 Write a short speech to your year group encouraging people to do something to save the planet. Remember to include some of the features you noted in Obama's speech.

You may choose to respond to your Spoken Language Study controlled assessment task by writing a story in which **direct speech** is a key focus. When writing dialogue for narrative writing, you should follow these conventions:

- Use the dialogue to create realistic characters, give different views on what is happening in the plot, and sometimes to move the plot forward.
- Use speech marks for dialogue embedded in narrative. For example, He turned to me. *"I'm hungry. Can we have lunch?"*
- Use words telling you who is speaking and how. For example, *"I'm hungry. Can we have lunch?" moaned John.*

ResultsPlus
Controlled assessment tip

If you are writing a story containing dialogue your readers need to know who said what. There is no need to use 'he said' or 'she said' after each piece of dialogue, but you need to take care that readers will understand what is happening.

Activity 2

Look at the passage below from *Of Mice and Men* by John Steinbeck, which uses dialogue to tell the story in place of narrative.

> Slim sat down on a box and George took his place opposite.
>
> 'It wasn't nothing,' said Slim. 'I would of had to drowned most of 'em, anyways. No need to thank me about that.'
>
> George said, 'It wasn't much to you, maybe, but it was a hell of a lot to him. Jesus Christ, I don't know how we're gonna get him to sleep in here. He'll want to sleep right out in the barn with 'em. We'll have trouble keepin' him from getting right in the box with them pups.'
>
> 'It wasn't nothing,' Slim repeated. 'Say, you sure was right about him. Maybe he ain't bright, but I never seen such a worker. He damn near killed his partner buckin' barley. There ain't nobody can keep up with him. God awmighty I never seen such a strong guy.'

1 **Find examples of the following conventions:**

a) speech marks
b) words indicating the speaker.

2 **Give two examples of how the dialogue reveals the personality of a character.**

3 **Give an example of how the dialogue tells the story.**

4 **Write a short section (no more than 10 lines) of a story with a focus on dialogue. It should include a conversation between two people discussing the issue of poor refereeing decisions made at football matches.**

8 Writing dialogue

This lesson will help you to...

→ **write realistic and effective dialogue**

To write a good script or narrative you must be able to write dialogue that is realistic. Ideas, setting and atmosphere are all important, but if the dialogue sounds strange and unrealistic the script will not be successful.

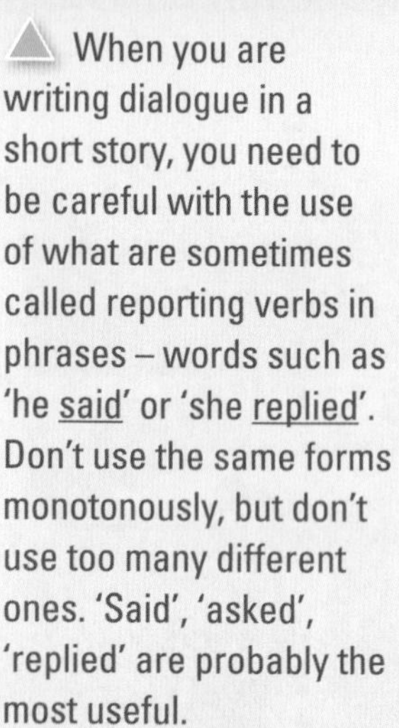

ResultsPlus
Controlled assessment tip

When you are writing dialogue in a short story, you need to be careful with the use of what are sometimes called reporting verbs in phrases – words such as 'he said' or 'she replied'. Don't use the same forms monotonously, but don't use too many different ones. 'Said', 'asked', 'replied' are probably the most useful.

Activity 1

Read the dialogue between two teenagers going to their form room at the beginning of the day. The school is the local comprehensive.

1 Explain what makes the dialogue unrealistic for its time, place and age contexts.

2 Rewrite the conversation to make the dialogue more realistic.

Andy: Morning old chap.

Dom: Hello Andy.

Andy: It's rather chilly this morning. I think I will put an extra sweater on when I take my little dog for a walk around the park this evening.

Dom: What a good idea. You don't want to catch a chill, do you?

To create successful dialogue you need to:

- Use an **appropriate register** for the situation. For example, if it is an interview the dialogue will be **formal**; if the conversation is between friends it will probably be **informal**, so you might include slang and dialect.
- Use **appropriate language** for the character and age of the person speaking. For example, you would not expect a pensioner to use teenage slang.
- Keep it quite **brief**. If a character has a lot to say their dialogue should be broken up by brief questions or comments from those listening.
- Ensure it has a **purpose**: for example, to develop the narrative, create atmosphere, or say more about a character and their motives.
- Ensure that the words and expressions used by the character reflect the **regional/cultural setting** of the story.

Notice how these techniques are used in the following extract from *Of Mice and Men*. It is a continuation of the extract you read in Lesson 7.

American dialect

Key insights into characters come from the conversation, not just a string of information from George.

George spoke proudly. 'Jus' tell Lennie what to do an' he'll do it if it don't take no figuring. He can't think of nothing to do himself, but he sure can take orders.'

There was a clang of horseshoe on iron stake outside and a little cheer of voices. Slim moved back slightly so the light was not on his face. 'Funny how you an' him string along together.' It was Slim's calm invitation to confidence.

'What's funny about it?' George demanded defensively.

'Oh, I dunno. Hardly none of the guys ever travel together. I hardly never seen two guys travel together. You know how the hands are, they just come in and get their bunk and work a month, and then they quit and go out alone. Never seem to give a damn about nobody. It jus' seems kinda funny a cuckoo like him and a smart little guy like you travellin' together.'

'He ain't no cuckoo,' said George. 'He's dumb as hell, but he ain't crazy. An' I ain't so bright neither, or I wouldn't be buckin' barley for my fifty and found. If I was bright, if I was even a little bit smart, I'd have my own little place, an' I'd be bringin' in my own crops, 'stead of doin' all the work and not getting what comes up outta the ground.' George fell silent. He wanted to talk. Slim neither encouraged nor discouraged him. He just sat back quiet and receptive.

Dialogue to build the character – shows that George and Lennie's relationship is unique.

Dialogue to build the character – shows that George is protective of Lennie.

'Hands' meaning 'workers' – appropriate vocabulary for working men.

Informal sentence structure provides suitable register for conversation between peers.

Activity 2

1 Write 100 to 150 words of a story with lots of direct speech. Ensure the dialogue:

a) uses an appropriate register for the situation
b) uses appropriate language for the character and age of the characters
c) has a purpose, e.g. to develop the narrative, create atmosphere or develop a character
d) reflects the regional/cultural setting of the story
e) is not too long – break it up with comments or questions from other characters.

ResultsPlus
Controlled assessment tip

In scripts and in narrative writing, dialogue can have several functions. The important ones are telling the story and creating character. You need to plan your dialogue carefully so that it performs these functions, but still seems realistic.

ResultsPlus
Build better answers

Look at this controlled assessment task:
Write a script that contains between 30 seconds and 2 minutes of spoken language for a TV drama

■ A Band 2 answer **expresses ideas that are sometimes appropriate**, shows **some understanding** of what you are writing and who you are writing for, with **some care in the choice of language** and the way it is put together.

Craig - Are we going out then?
Steve – I've got the car.
Sarah shouts Steve I got to talk to you
Craig – Get lost cow he doesn't want to see you
Sarah walks over to Steve You can't drive you've been drinking
Craig says - Get lost
Steve says leave me alone!

● A Band 3 answer expresses and **develops ideas appropriately**, shows a **clear understanding** of who you are writing for and why, uses **well-chosen vocabulary**, and shows some evidence of crafting in the construction of sentences.

Detective: Where were you the 18th July at 8.30 am?
Suspect: I was getting up, or on my way to work. I can't remember. Where were you?
Detective: (angry) You don't ask the questions. I do.
Suspect: Yeah, yeah.
Detective: We have you on CCTV talking to a man. That man was found murdered half an hour later.
Suspect: Well, I don't know anything about it.
Detective: What did you talk to him about?
Suspect: I don't remember.
Detective: (Stands up and bangs the table) What did you talk to him about!

▲ A Band 4 answer **effectively presents ideas in a sustained way**, and is written and structured in a way that is suitable for the chosen task, and for the appropriate audience. The words have been chosen with care and consideration, and the **writing is well-controlled**, with an **appropriate variety** in the construction of sentences.

Chris and Liam stare at a blue police box that has just materialised in the street in front of them.
Chris: Can you see it too?
Liam: I… don't know. Watch out!
The door opens and a man steps out. He looks puzzled.
Dr Who: You couldn't tell me where I am?
Liam: This is Bury. (Dr Who says nothing.)
Liam: In Lancashire. (Dr Who says nothing)
Liam: England.
Dr Who: Ah. Right. Very good. Now… Can you tell me what year it is?
Chris: Is this some kind of joke?
Dr Who: I wish it was.

Here is an example of a controlled assessment task you could be expected to answer.

You will be expected to write in the form of a script and will be expected to use the conventions of scripting.

Write a script that contains between 30 seconds and 2 minutes of spoken language for a TV soap.

(24 marks)

Activity 3

Write a response to this question:

Write the opening section of your first scene. You should focus on the conventions of a TV script.

You should spend 20 minutes on this question.

ResultsPlus
Self assessment

Before you do this self-assessment activity, you might like to read some sample answers to this task on the following pages (170-171).

1 Check your answer to Activity 3:

- Did you set your answer out using the proper conventions for a script?
- Did you include appropriate direction?
- Did you create realistic dialogue?
- Did you use the dialogue to create part of a story or narrative?

2 Now try to grade your answer to Activity 3 by applying the mark scheme opposite. You will need to be careful and precise in your marking.

Band 2

- script uses ideas that are sometimes appropriate for the task
- the writing is generally suitable for the audience
- includes dialogue that is sometimes effective
- the structure of the script is mostly appropriate

Band 3

- ideas are clearly expressed and suitable for the task
- the writing is mostly effective for the task and for the audience
- the dialogue is mostly realistic and effective for the story being created
- the script is properly structured with appropriate use of directions

Band 4

- ideas are clearly and effectively expressed
- the writing is very well planned for the task and for the audience
- the dialogue is realistic, develops the narrative and creates the appropriate effects
- the script is well-structured, and the directions help to set the scene and create the narrative

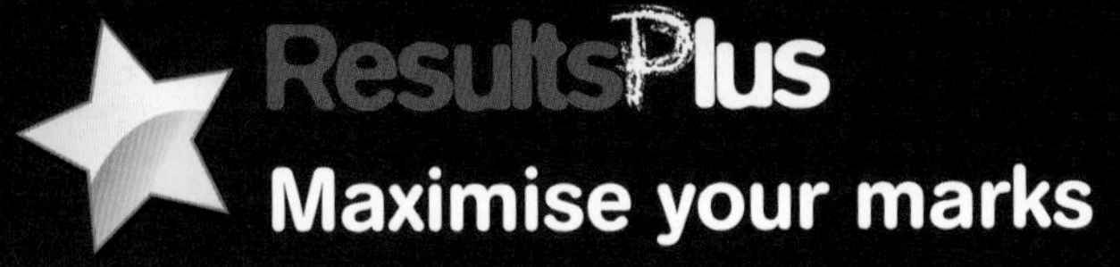

Write a script that contains between 30 seconds and 2 minutes of spoken language for a TV soap.

Here are three student answers to the writing about spoken language task on page 169. Read the answers together with the examiner comments around and after the answers. Then complete the activity.

Student 1 – Extract typical of a grade (D) answer

Vicky - what are you doing here

Sarah – walks over to Vicky

Sarah – I want a word with you you cow

Vicky swears at her

Vicky - Yeah what about

Sarah - You know

Attempt at screen directions.

This is not script.

Tries to create realistic dialogue.

Examiner summary

This part of the answer is typical of grade D performance. The student has created some realistic dialogue and set it out as a script with some success. The characters' spoken words are indicated in two places, but in one place, the script is written more like a short story. There is no setting or context, so the story that is developing here is not easy to identify.

Student 2 – Extract typical of a grade (C) answer

(In the interview room)

Stevie: OK, Jack, the interview starts here.

Neil: This is your last chance, Jack. You can tell us your version.

Jack: what do you mean? I told you the truth.

Neil: So you say.

Jack: Don't get clever with me (stands up)

Neil: Don't try anything, I'm warning you.

(Jack tries to hit him)

Opening sets the scene.

Realistic dialogue.

Scene moves a bit too fast.

Examiner summary

This part of the answer is typical of grade C performance. The student has set this out as a script, and has given some context so the developing story is easier to identify. The dialogue is in the appropriate form for a script, and there is a good attempt to make it realistic. However, the action moves a bit too fast. It might be better to have a little more development before the fight.

Student 3 – Extract typical of a grade B answer

Dialogue sets the scene well.

Scene: (exterior, wide angles) Street at night. Passers-by. BEN waits by the bus stop for AISHA. He's looking at his watch.

Aisha: (Running towards him) Sorry, I'm sorry.

Ben: What happened?

Aisha: I couldn't get away. I think they might have guessed.

Ben: (Looks round nervously) Did anyone see you go?

Aisha: (Looks round as well) No. said I was going to the shop.

Ben: We've got to get out of here.

Dialogue gives important narrative information.

Examiner summary

This part of the answer is typical of grade B performance. The script is set out using appropriate conventions and uses enough screen direction to make it clear exactly what is happening. The dialogue is realistic and shows a developing story and developing tension, without moving too fast.

ResultsPlus

Build better answers

Move from a Grade D to Grade C

In this part of your task you need to set your answer out like a script. You need to give appropriate directions and use realistic dialogue to develop your characters. You should keep your story in mind and make sure your script is following this.

Move from a Grade C to Grade B

The difference between Student 2 and Student 3 is that Student 3 uses enough direction to make it clear what is happening. She manages to create a tense situation through dialogue, and she doesn't move the story on too fast. The dialogue is realistic and the characters are believable and well-developed.

Putting it into Practice

1 **Working in groups, perform your scripts. Is your script effective when it is read out?**

2 **Make notes of what was effective in the scripts, and what didn't work so well.**

Controlled Assessment Practice

Examiner's tip

You need two examples. Try to think of two that are interesting to you and will give you material to discuss in your assessment.

Examiner's tip

You will need to comment on context and choice.

Guidance for students: Spoken Language Study

What do I have to do?
You will complete one task on spoken language, from a choice of two. You must complete this task on your own.

How much time do I have?
Following preparation and research, you will have up to two hours to complete the task.

How do I prepare for the task?
You must research examples of spoken language. These may include:

- the language you hear around you
- a selection which could be taken from sources such as YouTube, TV or radio interviews, radio phone-ins, soap operas or the British Library audio archives
- your or your school's own recorded materials.

You must provide two examples of spoken language to complete the chosen task. These examples can be taken from any of the sources.

What must my response to the task show?
Your responses must show that you:

- understand how spoken language changes depending on the context, using examples
- understand some of the choices people make when they are speaking (for example: how they say it; what words or phrases they choose), using examples.

How should I present my response?
The response must allow you to show understanding of the examples of spoken language chosen. The response will be a written response of up to 1000 words to the task.

The Spoken Language Study Task for the Student

You will complete one task from the two below:

EITHER
Using two examples of spoken language, comment on the way teenagers adapt their spoken language to suit the situation.

You should comment on:
- how the purpose of the spoken language affects the way it is used
- how language use influences other speakers and listeners
- the level of formality
- the use of slang
- who speaks most if there is more than one speaker. (24)

OR
Using two examples of spoken language, comment on the differences between the speech of the area where you live and the speech of different places. (You may comment on ONE other place or more if you choose.)

You should comment on:
- how the purpose of the spoken language affects the way it is used
- how language use influences other speakers and listeners
- the level of formality
- the use of slang
- who speaks most if there is more than one speaker. (24)

Examiner's tip

Pick one of these tasks. Try to focus on language that interests you.

Examiner's tip

Use these bullets to help you form and structure your response.

Guidance for students: Writing for the Spoken Voice

What do I have to do?
You will complete one task from a choice of three.

You must complete this task on your own.

How much time do I have?
Following preparation and research, you will have up to two hours to complete this task.

How do I prepare for the task?
You should watch, read and listen to examples of the way writers create spoken words. These may include:

- radio plays
- films
- TV drama
- radio and TV documentaries
- sitcoms
- radio advertisements
- graphic novels
- monologues
- speeches
- stand-up comedy.

What must the response to the task show?
The response must show that you:
- understand how a media type (radio, TV, graphic novels, etc) works
- understand the needs of an audience and purpose.

How should I present the response?
As a written response that is effective for the form, purpose and audience chosen for the task.

Writing for the Spoken Voice Task for the Student

You will complete one task from those below:

EITHER
Write a script that contains between 30 seconds and 2 minutes of spoken language for:

- a TV soap **OR**
- a graphic novel **OR**
- a radio drama.

Your script may be totally original **OR** may be for a TV soap, graphic novel or radio drama that already exists.

(24)

OR
Write a speech of up to 1000 words in support of a topic of your choice in a debate.

(24)

OR
Write a story of up to 1000 words in which direct speech is a key focus.

(24)

Examiner's tip

Select one task from these three. Use your creativity to make your spoken language interesting.

Examiner's tip

Remember to make your spoken language appropriate for the form you're writing in.

Published by Pearson Education Limited, a company incorporated in England and Wales, having its registered office at Edinburgh Gate, Harlow, Essex, CM20 2JE. Registered company number: 872828

Edexcel is a registered trade mark of Edexcel Limited

First published 2010

12 11 10
10 9 8 7 6 5 4 3 2 1

British Library Cataloguing in Publication Data
A catalogue record for this book is available from the British Library

ISBN 978 1 84690 703 6

Designed and typeset by Juice Creative Limited, Hertfordshire
Printed and bound in Great Britain at Scotprint, Haddington

Picture Credits
The publisher would like to thank the following for their kind permission to reproduce their photographs:
(Key: b-bottom; c-centre; l-left; r-right; t-top)
akg-images Ltd: M.G.M / Album 165, Michael Mathias Prechtl 129; **Alamy Images:** Shoosh / Form Advertising 53, Shoosh / Form Advertising 53, KBG, allOver 10, blickwinkel 28, H Armstrong Roberts, ClassicStock 155, Kathy deWitt 9, Jeff Morgon built environment 131, 137, Tyler Durden / FogStock 72, GlowImages11 154, Roberto Herrett 97, Imagebroker 15, Kelly Redinger / Designs Pics Inc 145, Leah Warkentin, Design Pics Inc. 65, Jon Arnold Images Ltd 28 (2), Roland Nagy 66, Nikreates 57l, AR Photo 152, Matthieu Spohn / PhotoAlto 135, Ian West, Bubbles Photolibrary 90, Skyscan Photolibrary 28 (3), IS784, Image Source Pink 73, RTimages 96, 156, Jim Wileman 102 (2); **Camera Press Ltd:** Robert Doisneau 142; **Corbis:** Tim Pannell 94; **The Decatur Daily:** Gary Cosby Jr. 29; **FremantleMedia Stills Library:** TalkbackThames / SYCO TV 89 (2); **Getty Images:** 103, Tim Boyle 120, Cate Gillon 11, Ferdaus Shamim 74t, Tom Shaw 34 (2), AFP / Stringer 35br, Ben Stansall / Stringer 142 (2), Mark Thompson 57l (2), Michael Turek 102; **iStockphoto:** 17, 81, 122 (3), 122 (4), 124, David Foreman 34, 143 (2), John Freeman 158, Chris Hepburn 148, Elena Korenbaum 122, Brian Moore 124 (2), Patricia Nelson 88, Chris Price 98, Graeme Purdy 117, Hasan Shaheed 115, Alexandr Vlassyuk 147 (2); **Kobal Collection Ltd:** 30, Maverick Films 136; **National Geographic:** Paul Nicklen 29 (2); **Pearson Education Ltd:** Gareth Boden 84, Photodisc. Steve Cole 44, Photodisc. Kevin Peterson 151, Photodisc 87, 147, Brand X Pictures. Burke Triolo Productions 66 (2), Steve Shott 89, Studio 8. Clark Wiseman 15 (2), 70, 71, 166, Studio 8. Clark Wiseman 15 (2), 70, 71, 166, Studio 8. Clark Wiseman 15 (2), 70, 71, 166, Studio 8. Clark Wiseman 15 (2), 70, 71, 166; **Inpho Photography:** 74b; **Photolibrary.com:** Index Stock Imagery 68, Light Artist Photography 146; **Press Association:** Yui Mok 82, Michael Stephens 57r (3); **Reuters:** Anthony Harvey 74, Atef Hassan 122 (2), Stephen Hird 104, Brendan McDermid 105, Jason Reed 164; **shutterstock:** Alan Morgan 154 (2); **Veer:** Martin Crowdy 143; **Esteve Lopez, www.lostlandscapes.com:** 116
Cover images: *Front:* **iStockphoto:** Krzysztof Kwiatkowski

All other images © Pearson Education

Every effort has been made to trace the copyright holders and we apologise in advance for any unintentional omissions. We would be pleased to insert the appropriate acknowledgement in any subsequent edition of this publication.

Acknowledgements
We are grateful to the following for permission to reproduce copyright material:
Logos. Logo on page 34 from The England and Wales Cricket Board, © 1997-2005 England and Wales Cricket Board Limited (ECB). ECB, cricket ball imagery, the 3 lions logo and ECB logo are trade marks (or where relevant registered trade marks) of the ECB.
Screenshots. Screenshot on page 12 from 'Bullying, it's hard to piece your life back together!!!' poster, http://www.rawmarshclc.org.uk/dc/ppxbullying/pictures/1.jpg, Rawmarsh City Learning Centre; Screenshot on page 12 from 'Why do people bully?' poster, http://www.didax.com/support/images/2-166/2-166a.gif, Didax, Inc; Screenshot on page 14 from *Freshwater Fishing Australia* Issue 89, March/April 2008, http://www.afn.com.au, artwork of cover of *Freshwater Fishing Australia* magazine reproduced with permission from Australian Fishing Network; Screenshot on page 14 from *Cosmopolitan*, March 2008, Cosmopolitan Magazine, The National Magazine Company; Screenshot on page 14 from *BeanoMax*, No. 1, 15 February 2007, Beanomax © D.C.Thomson & Co., Ltd; Screenshot on page 21 from *Exploring Science: How Science Works, Year 9 Pupil Book*, Pearson Education Ltd (Levesley, M. 2009) pp. 108-109; Screenshot on page 22 from leaflet 'Mayday Mayday. Invasion of the Climate Snatchers', www.risingtide.org.uk, Rising Tide; Screenshot on page 22 from leaflet 'Global Warming?', The Heartland Institute, http://www.heartland.org/; Screenshots on page 23, page 31, page 41 from http://www.eurotrip.com, EuroTrip.com; Screenshot on page 26 from Crimestoppers homepage, www.crimestoppers-uk.org; Screenshot on page 27 from cover of Crimestoppers leaflet 'Crime & Your Community', www.crimestoppers-uk.org; Screenshot on page 29 from PlayStation3 cover shot - Tom Clancy's H.A.W.X., with permission from Ubisoft; Screenshot on page 36 from 'Top fire safety tips', http://firekills.direct.gov.uk/fire-safety-quick-guide.html, Department of Communities and Local Government; Screenshot on page 37 from Children's Burns Trust leaflet, Children's Burns Trust. Leaflet, and 'Hot Water Burns Like Fire' image and wording are used by permission of Reliance Water Controls Ltd; Screenshot on page 37 from video Ash 2008, http://firekills.direct.gov.uk/video.html, Department of Communities and Local Government; Screenshot on page 39 from Innocent Smoothies poster, January 2007 advertising campaign, Innocent Ltd; Screenshot on page 40 from MBT the anti-shoe poster, Masai GB Ltd., www.mbt.com; Screenshot on page 46 from I Like Music, http://www.ilikemusic.com, with permission from I Like Music; Screenshot on page 46 from *NME*, cover September 2006, © Andy Whitton/NME/IPC+ Syndication; Screenshot on page 51 from Greenpeace Climate Change, http://www.greenpeace.org.uk/climate, Greenpeace UK; Screenshot on page 56 from *Doctor Who Adventures*, Issue 65, 22-28 May 2008, Cover image © BBC Worldwide; Screenshot on page 58 from What's wrong with crating?, http://www.petaliterature.com/prodinfo.asp?number=WEL253, peta.org; Screenshot on page 58 from 7 Excellent iPhone Apps for Dog Lovers by Mary Ward, The Daily Woof, posted 21 September 2009, http://www.thedailywoof.blogspot.com/, reproduced with permission from Mary Ward, WriteAndWorkonline.com; Screenshots on page 58, page 86 from *Okehampton Times*, 3 September 2009, No. 1720, Reproduced courtesy of the Okehampton Times; Screenshot on page 86 from Transition Town Totnes, http://totnes.transitionnetwork.org; Screenshot on page 104 from *The Penguin Guide to Punctuation*, Penguin (Larry Trask, ed. 1997), Copyright © Penguin Books, 1997; Screenshot on page 126 from *The Tar Man*, Simon and Schuster Children's Books (Buckley-Archer, L. 2007), Cover by